# ESSENTIAL MESSAGES
## FOR YOUTH MINISTRY

[20 POWERFUL YOUTH TALKS]

## Group

Loveland, Colorado
www.group.com

# Group resources actually work!

This Group resource helps you focus on **"The 1 Thing"**—a life-changing relationship with Jesus Christ. "The 1 Thing" incorporates our **R.E.A.L.** approach to ministry. It reinforces a growing friendship with Jesus, encourages long-term learning, and results in life transformation, because it's:

**Relational**
Learner-to-learner interaction enhances learning and builds Christian friendships.

**Experiential**
What learners experience through discussion and action sticks with them up to 9 times longer than what they simply hear or read.

**Applicable**
The aim of Christian education is to equip learners to be both hearers and doers of God's Word.

**Learner-based**
Learners understand and retain more when the learning process takes into consideration how they learn best.

## Essential Messages for Youth Ministry

Copyright © 2006 Group Publishing, Inc.

Visit our Web site: www.group.com

## CREDITS

Contributing Authors: Kent Julian, James W. Miller, Doc Newcomb, Siv M. Ricketts, Christina Schofield, Kelli B. Trujillo

Editor: Debbie Gowensmith

Acquisitions Editor: Kate S. Holburn

Creative Development Editor: Mikal Keefer

Chief Creative Officer: Joani Schultz

Copy Editor: Mary Ann Jeffreys

Art Director/Designer: Sharon Anderson

Print Production Artists: Joyce Douglas, Pat Reinheimer

Handout Illustrator: Matt Wood

Production Manager: Dodie Tipton

## Library of Congress Cataloging-in-Publication Data

Essential messages for youth ministry.--1st American pbk. ed.
      p. cm.
Includes index.
ISBN 0-7644-3078-5 (pbk. : alk. paper)
1. Christian education of teenagers. 2. Christian education--Activity programs. I. Group Publishing.
BV1485.E87 2005
268' .433--dc22            2005023801

10 9 8 7 6 5 4 3 2       15 14 13 12 11 10 09 08 07 06
Printed in the United States of America

# Contents

# Contributors

Many thanks to the following people, who regularly offer their creativity to impact youth for Jesus, for their wonderful contributions to this book.

**Kent Julian,** National Director for Alliance Youth in Atlanta, Georgia

**James W. Miller,** Associate Pastor at First Presbyterian Church in Honolulu, Hawaii

**Doc Newcomb,** Camp Services Program Manager at Group Workcamps in Loveland, Colorado

**Siv M. Ricketts,** Student Ministries Director in San Diego, California

**Christina Schofield,** junior high Sunday school teacher at Ridgeview Christian Church in Rolla, Missouri

**Kelli B. Trujillo,** writer, editor, and youth ministry volunteer in Indianapolis, IN; co-author of *Jesus— the Life Changer*, published by Group Publishing, Inc.

# Introduction

Messages have long been a mainstay of youth ministry. We just can't live without 'em. But can you remember sitting through messages that lulled you to sleep or caused you to wonder, *What does this have to do with MY life?* We know you don't want your youth to be thinking just about your messages!

That's what's different about *Essential Messages for Youth Ministry*. Each message centers on a topic that is totally relevant to teenagers' lives...today...here and now. To take it further, these messages don't present the topics in the same ol' heard-it-all-before kind of way. These messages are *experiential*.

## Keeping It R.E.A.L.

This is all part of what we call R.E.A.L. Learning—learning that's relational, experiential, active, learner-based, and life-changing. People who know teenagers well—people like those who contributed to this book—understand that the best growth takes place in a nurturing and suitable environment. Study after study, in addition to casual conversations and your own life experiences, demonstrates that people don't retain information or experience a life change by simply sitting and listening to someone talk. You can deliver the most impassioned, most profound message of your life, but its impact will be limited if you ask your teenagers to just sit through it.

Don't despair, though, because *Essential Messages for Youth Ministry* provides a solution. These messages are interspersed with dynamic, hands-on activities that directly involve your teenagers in the topics. Creating clogs to learn about sin, practicing "about face" maneuvers to learn about repentance, smelling the enticing aroma of pizza to learn about sexual temptation, creating "villains" to learn about forgiveness—no matter what learning style a student most responds to, he or she will find it here. In-depth discussions that push way beyond yes-no answers also provide challenge, inspiration, and increased understanding.

If you're afraid that active learning may distract from biblical truth, just thumb through a few messages. They are based squarely on Scripture. Each message leads teenagers to explore what the Bible really has to say about the topic; the experiences simply help to drive home the truths that Scripture provides.

The combination of active learning, meaningful discussions, and biblical truth that you'll find in these essential messages all lead teenagers to The One Thing, the most important thing: a growing, thriving, exciting friendship with Jesus.

# Here's What You'll Find in Each Message

As you peruse a message, you'll notice italicized type and regular type. Directions to you are set in *italics,* the words you'll speak directly to your group are set in regular type, and discussion questions are **boldfaced.** In addition, you'll find the following sections in each message.

**TOPIC:** As you may have guessed, this is the subject that a particular message will explore. We think you'll agree that these topics are incredibly relevant to what your teenagers experience in their lives and in their relationships with Christ.

**SCRIPTURE:** Your students will delve deeply into these Bible verses.

**PURPOSE:** This summarizes the message's goal—the result you'll see in students' lives.

**SUPPLIES NEEDED:** We know you're busy. You don't have time to sort through pages and pages in order to figure out what supplies you need. No worries. We've listed everything you need right up front.

**SET-UP:** Ditto. This is everything you'll need to do ahead of time.

**STARTING OFF:** This section introduces the topic and draws in even your most sleepy, reluctant, and antsy students.

**DIGGING IN:** The "meat" of the message, this section plunges teenagers into Scripture for an in-depth, active exploration of the topic.

**WRAPPING UP:** This finishing touch rounds out the message and drives home the key points.

**DAILY CHALLENGE®:** This is where your teenagers commit to real, everyday things they can do to grow spiritually. These messages don't let teenagers get away without asking them to live out what they've learned in very specific and meaningful ways during the coming days.

**BONUS IDEAS:** These are found in each message and provide something you can do if you want to reach a whole new level of creativity.

**TIPS FOR THE LEADER:** We think your growth as a leader is important, so we've provided tips that either contribute to your leadership skills or specifically help you make the most of the message.

**PARENT CONNECT BOX:** Your relationship with your students' parents is key. These boxes provide great ideas for reaching out to parents, encouraging parents and their teenagers to grow together, and more.

Finally, you'll notice that the messages are arranged in alphabetical order by topic; a quick glance at the Contents will help you find the message that corresponds with just the topic you want to teach. And if you'd rather find a message that incorporates a particular Scripture, well, you can do that, too. Just check the Scripture Index at the back of the book.

# We Saved the Best for Last!

*Essential Messages for Youth Ministry* includes a totally cool, totally useful ministry tool that will pump energy and creativity into these messages. The *Essential Messages* CD includes 12 audio tracks and 16 pdf files that will engage your students. The audio tracks will help teenagers learn and explore God's truths in a way that they understand and are comfortable with. And the pdf files provide 16 handouts that are incorporated into the other active-learning components of the messages. Awesome, huh?

# Have Fun!

Now it's time for the fun part—choosing a message to use with your group. You'll find that these messages fit groups from five to fifty-five, especially given the Tips for the Leader that suggest modifications for smaller or larger groups. We encourage you to adapt, morph, and piece together these messages in any creative way you can. Choose two activities and scrap the third, or blend two messages to fit your exact goals. Use these messages for meetings, retreats, campouts, small groups—any way you like. They're written to be flexible and fun. Most of all, they're written to be *used*. Our sincere hope is that this book will become one of the most dog-eared and coffee-stained books on your desk!

# About the Use of Video Clips

According to federal copyright laws, rented or personal videos cannot be used for any purpose other than home viewing. In order to show a video clip in your youth ministry, it's best to obtain a license. For more information about copyright laws or to obtain a blanket license for a small fee, contact the Motion Picture Licensing Corporation at www.mplc.com or call 1-800-462-8855.

Also when using a video clip, it's critical that you preview the clip before you use it. Not only will such preparation ensure that your equipment is working correctly, but it also allows you to screen out any material you consider inappropriate for your particular group.

# God's Body

*12/4/11*

## TOPIC
**Alcohol and Drugs**

## SCRIPTURE
- Psalm 139:13-16
- Mark 12:28-30
- Romans 12:1-2
- 1 Thessalonians 5:23

## PURPOSE
To encourage students to commit to God-honoring choices regarding alcohol and drugs.

## SUPPLIES NEEDED
- *Essential Messages* CD
- CD player
- Bibles
- Scissors, newsprint, markers, and masking tape
- Newsboys *Devotion* CD
- Paper and pens

## SET-UP
- Cut enough 6-foot pieces of newsprint for every three to five people to have one piece.
- Set up the CD player with the *Essential Messages* CD cued to audio track 1, "My Walk on the Wild Side."
- Have the Newsboys *Devotion* CD ready to play "I Love Your Ways" (track 2).

---

### BONUS IDEA

If someone in your church teaches aerobics or other fitness classes, ask that person to lead your group in a time of physical activity. Be sure your volunteer mentions that we can honor and praise God through physical fitness.

## Starting Off
### Seduced!

 *Ask teenagers to reflect on what they know about alcohol and drugs and what they or others have experienced as you play audio track 1 from the* Essential Messages *CD, "My Walk on the Wild Side." Afterward, lead a discussion.*

*Ask*
- **What from this story most struck you? Why?**
- **What makes alcohol and drugs so appealing?**

TV shows, movies, music, video games, magazines—media sources often portray fun, popularity, and alcohol hand-in-hand. These sources rarely highlight the dangers of indulging. The image of alcohol and drugs portrayed in the media and the overwhelming stress people feel today through difficult life circumstances combine to create a recipe for potential drug and alcohol abuse.

*Ask*

- **If media sources were totally truthful about alcohol and drugs, what kinds of scenes would they portray?**

Today we'll look at a more honest perspective on drugs and alcohol. We'll especially focus on the biblical view of our bodies, which can help us decide what to do when faced with the temptation to drink or do drugs.

*For two or three minutes, lead students in some basic stretches to get their blood flowing, release tension, get them to pay attention to their bodies, and focus on the topic.*

# Digging In
## Your Body Is a Gift From God

*Give each small group a 6-foot piece of newsprint and markers. Have groups trace one person's body on the newsprint. This will represent everyone's body. Then instruct small groups to read Psalm 139:13-16 together.*

*Afterward, ask small groups to write inside their body outlines words or phrases from the passage (or ideas the passage evokes for them) that convey the gift we have received from God via our bodies. For example, groups might write, "fearfully and wonderfully made" or "strong and healthy." After a few minutes, ask groups to share their drawings.*

Consider this illustration: Your parents give you an extremely valuable gift for Christmas—one you've been hoping for. This is not your run-of-the-mill present, but a very special one. You jump up and down and scream when you open it, and you call all your friends to share your awesome news. But after you enjoy the gift for a while, you begin to take it for granted. A little while later, you don't even notice that you're walking on it as it lies on your bedroom floor. The gift is still as valuable and awesome as ever. It hasn't changed, but you've forgotten just how special it is.

Now magnify that special gift to the umpteenth degree, and that's the gift of your body—that God's given you. The Bible says God knit us together, carefully crafting each part of each one of us with a reverent attitude for the work being done. God gave us our bodies so that we could live fully, enjoy the gift of life, and honor God with everything we are.

*Have small groups discuss the following questions. (For all the questions you come to in the "Digging In" section, have small groups discuss them.)*

*Ask*

- **When you think about your body's being a gift from God, what's your response? Why?**

- **What do you think it's like for God to see the people he created hurting their bodies?**
- **How would thinking of your body as a gift from God affect your desire to drink or do drugs? Explain.**

Most of us take our bodies for granted until something goes wrong. Say you pull a muscle and can't move the way you're used to without a lot of pain. That's when you realize just how important your body is and just how much you need even the smallest muscle.

Think about how sad you might feel if you saw your friend absentmindedly damaging a gift you'd given her. Imagine how God must hurt when we abuse the bodies so tenderly and lovingly made for us. When we use and abuse alcohol and drugs, we can do great harm to our bodies.

## Your Body Is an Offering to God

There is an alternative, of course. We can choose to recognize God's gift of our bodies and respond by presenting our bodies as an offering to God.

*Ask for a volunteer to read aloud Romans 12:1-2.*

Paul urges, encourages, pleads with us to treat our bodies with respect. He asks, "When you consider how huge God's mercy is, isn't it reasonable that we should respond by giving God full control of our lives, including our bodies?" God gives us physical life and spiritual life, wants to have a relationship with us, and forgives us even though we don't deserve it. When we recognize what God has done for us, then we humbly offer what God wants most—our whole selves, bodies included—and try to live in a way that honors God.

## The Mind-Body Connection

*Ask for a volunteer to read aloud Mark 12:28-30.*

Heart, soul, mind, and strength. In other words, emotions, spirit, thoughts, and body. That's everything you are! When we love God, we give him our all without holding anything back because it's all connected.

What we do with our minds affects our bodies. Athletes know the importance of training their minds in order to get their bodies to work better. Likewise, what we do with our bodies affects our minds and spirits.

Say you have a few drinks at a party this weekend. At the next party, it'll be even easier to have a few. Your body will get used to it, and so will your mind. Or say you get your body to church week after week, whether or not you feel like it. After a while, the physical habit of being here will probably seep into your mind and affect what you think about church. Try this: Smile, right now, even if you don't feel like it. Keep smiling.

All teenagers are at risk of using alcohol and drugs. Use whatever venues you have for communicating with parents—for example, your own letters to parents, the church newsletter or bulletin, or parent meetings—to encourage parents to become as knowledgeable as they can on the issue.

Web pages such as the one posted by the American Academy of Child & Adolescent Psychiatry can prove helpful in identifying those at risk and noticing warning signs. Check it out at http://www.aacap.org /publications/factsfam/teendrug .htm.

You might consider hosting an occasional parent discussion group and inviting a speaker—a mental health professional, a school administrator or counselor, a doctor, or someone from Alcoholics Anonymous—to address and equip parents with preventative care ideas.

Then smile some more. After a while, you'll find yourself feeling happier. Where your body goes, your mind follows. God wants your words, emotions, spirit, thoughts, and body to follow him.

*Ask*

- **What's an example from your own life of the mind-body connection—perhaps a time when doing something with your body affected the way you thought or felt about something?**

- **How do you think using drugs or alcohol could affect your ability to follow God with all your heart, soul, mind, and strength?**

## God's on Your Side

*Ask for a volunteer to read aloud 1 Thessalonians 5:23.*

The really good news is that you're not alone. God is at work in us and can help us make good choices about what we feed our bodies. Of course, people who choose to love and follow Jesus aren't instantly made perfect. We're still tempted, and we still blow it. But as we turn to God with our whole selves, he works in us to help us stand strong against temptations like drugs and alcohol.

*Ask*

- **In what ways can we present our bodies as offerings to God?**

- **How would offering your body to God affect your desire to drink and do drugs? Explain.**

*Ask small groups to review the Scripture passages and write on their body outlines words or phrases that convey the offering we give to God in our bodies. For example, groups might write, "love God with all your strength" or "blameless." After a few minutes, ask groups to share.*

# Wrapping Up

It can be so difficult to stand against peer pressure. You can know all the facts about how bad substance abuse is for your body and the potentially deadly consequences, but at some point you may just have to trust that God's ways are better for you and rely on God to help you not give in.

*Ask students to listen for two things in a song you're going to play: (1) How trusting God can help them resist temptation to drink or do drugs, and (2) how they can present their bodies as offerings to God (for example, by using their eyes to read God's Word or using their ears to listen to their youth leaders and Christian friends).*

*Play "I Love Your Ways," which is track 2 off the Newsboys* Devotion *CD. Let groups write their observations on their body outlines, and after a few minutes, have groups share what they wrote.*

*Pray*

God loves us so much that he gave us an amazing gift: life. That life comes packaged in our physical bodies. We can choose to live our lives by the world's rules and lies, or we can choose to love God's ways. This includes remembering that our bodies are gifts from God and then letting our actions mirror that amazing truth. We can choose to honor God with our bodies, which will help us to resist the appeal of alcohol and drugs.

## DAILY CHALLENGE®

*Remind students of the story from the CD they heard at the beginning of this message (if necessary, play it again). Pass out paper and pens, and ask students to write the narrator a letter, putting into practice what they learned today. As part of the letter, have teenagers write one thing they will commit to doing in the next few days to present their bodies as offerings to God and resist the temptation to use alcohol and drugs.*

*Before students leave, remind them to follow through on their Daily Challenge commitment—and to tell someone how it goes.*

### TIP FOR THE LEADER

Put up in your meeting room the outlines teenagers drew on the newsprint to remind them of what they learned during this message.

# Working Through the Word

## TOPIC
**The Bible**

## SCRIPTURE
- 2 Kings 23:1-3, 25
- 2 Timothy 3:16-17
- Hebrews 4:12

## PURPOSE
To help students realize that the Bible is living and active and to encourage them to rely on it for every part of their lives.

## SUPPLIES NEEDED
- *Essential Messages* CD
- CD player
- Bibles
- Paper and pen for every four students
- TV, VCR/DVD player, and *Luther* video/DVD (Metro-Goldwyn-Mayer, 2003)
- Bible concordances, dictionaries, and other references

## SET-UP
- Set up the CD player with the *Essential Messages* CD cued to track 2, "Three Conversations."

- Print enough copies of the "Quotable Quotes" from the *Essential Messages* CD so that every two or three students has a copy.

- Print enough copies of the "Family Life" devotional from the *Essential Messages* CD so that each student has one.

- Set up a TV and VCR/DVD player, and cue *Luther* to 15:86:23 (if you're using a VCR, set the counter to 0:00:00 when the studio logo appears). Preview the clip at least once before teenagers arrive.

## BONUS IDEA

Use the "Quotable Quotes" downloadable file from the *Essential Messages* CD to create an overhead transparency or a PowerPoint slide. Project the quotes on a wall with an overhead projector or a computer during this activity.

## Starting Off
### Living and Active

*Have teenagers get into groups of four, and distribute paper and a pen to each group.*

Let's see how many documents or books you can list that actually affect your life today in some way. For example, the Constitution of the United States affects the laws that govern you, certain books influence the way you think, and even a traffic ticket is a document that affects you.

*Allow groups a few minutes to brainstorm, and then have them share their lists. Afterward, have a volunteer read aloud 2 Timothy 3:16-17.*

*Then lead a short discussion.*

*Ask*

- **In what ways do these documents affect you?**

- **How is the Bible similar to and different from these other documents?**

- **What does it mean to you that the Bible is God-breathed?**

Today we're going to consider what it means that the Bible is living and active, affecting us in new ways each day. We'll think about how, through God's Word, we can meet Jesus personally.

# Digging In
## The Bible Is Different From Other Sources

 *Gather everyone together for this activity. Distribute copies of the "Quotable Quotes" so that everyone can see them (for instance, giving one copy to every second or third person). Have different volunteers read aloud different quotes, and then lead a short discussion.*

*Ask*

- **What's your general reaction to quotes from the Bible? to quotes from other sources?**

- **What's the difference in authority between the Bible and writings from other moral teachers or historical documents? Explain.**

- **How has the Bible's influence been different than anyone else's influence?**

Many of us have a different emotional reaction to teachings from the Bible when compared to teachings from other sources. Sometimes we respond positively to the Bible, especially when we read something we've heard before or something that makes sense to us.

Sometimes we have a negative reaction to the Bible—perhaps when it encourages us to do something difficult or when we don't understand it.

But for people who've discovered or grown in a relationship with Jesus through the Bible, it's more than just another big religious or historical text. It's a book we dig into and seek to understand. It's a book written with greater authority than books written by other human beings. We look to it for guidance about the most important things in our lives. We read it to grow closer to our Creator and our wonderful friend—Jesus.

## The Bible Is Powerful

Throughout history, people have believed so much in the power of the Bible to change lives that they have put great effort into translating it into thousands of languages. We're going to watch part of the story of a man who translated the Bible into German so that people could read it for themselves. The man's name is Martin Luther, and he got into a lot of trouble with the church in Germany at the time because he didn't have permission to translate the Bible.

*Show the clip from* Luther, *from 15:86:23 to 15:87:37, which depicts a brief conversation Luther had with a friend. After the clip, turn off the VCR/DVD player and the TV.*

*Have a volunteer read aloud Hebrews 4:12, and then lead a discussion.*

*Ask*

- **What's your reaction to this clip?**

- **Why do you think it's so important to some people that the Bible be translated into every language?**

- **What do you think this verse in Hebrews means when it refers to the Bible as being "living and active"? as being "sharper than any double-edged sword"?**

- **Have you experienced the Bible the way it's described in Hebrews? If so, how?**

The Bible isn't a book to be read lightly, a novel about a bunch of perfect people and their warm, fuzzy faith. It's powerful—living, active, sharp, and penetrating.

It records the stories of people and communities throughout history who have done good and evil, who have succeeded and failed, who have loved God and hated God. In all the lives we read about in the Bible, God was intimately involved—just as God is involved in my life and your life.

The Bible is powerful because we can know God better by reading how he interacted with the complex people and communities recorded there. The Bible is powerful because as we read, God teaches us about our own responsibilities, strengths, weaknesses, and brokenness.

The Bible is powerful because the Holy Spirit uses it to speak to each of us uniquely, depending upon what we've been through and what we're dealing with today. The Bible is powerful because it teaches us and leads us. No wonder it's so important that this "living and active" Word be translated into all languages!

## The Bible Is a Real Book for Real Life

Think about the way you make decisions. Whom do you consult? Where do you go for advice? How might Jesus play a part in your decision making? The Bible can serve as a practical source of advice for some

important choices. Let's experiment with how the Bible can help with some real-life situations. As you listen, think about how the Bible might address the issues these people face.

*Play track 2 of the* Essential Messages *CD, "Three Conversations."*

*Then have teenagers form groups of three or four for a discussion, and be sure each group has a Bible.*

*Ask*

• **Based on what you know or what you've heard about the Bible, how could the Bible impact each of these people's situations?**

Think about a similar situation in your own life—a tough decision you need to make or something you want to better understand.

*Ask*

• **How might you turn to the Bible to handle what you're facing in your own life?**

Even the Bible itself shows how Scripture can affect people's lives. The Old Testament explains how Moses wrote down the laws God had given to the Israelites. But then for years and years, those laws were lost. Israel's kings led their people to worship idols and do some pretty horrible things to one another. Then when a young man named Josiah was king, God's law was found.

*In their groups, have teenagers read 2 Kings 23:1-3, 25 and then discuss the following questions:*

*Ask*

• **What impact did finding God's law have on Josiah?**

• **Why do you think the Bible has such an impact on people's everyday lives?**

• **How might your life be different if the Bible was a bigger part of it?**

# Wrapping Up

The Bible is living and active. Unlike other texts and moral teachers, the Bible has endured the tests of history to remain a powerful influence on the way we think. When we apply the Bible to our lives, it has the power to capture our attention, challenge us to grow, and even change us.

One way we can apply the Bible is to more deeply learn how to use it. Studying the Bible is a lifelong pursuit, and we can involve useful tools in the process.

*Distribute a concordance, Bible dictionary, or other reference to each group. Have groups each choose a topic that's relevant to their lives, look it up in the reference, and then read at least two to three accompanying Scriptures.*

# DAILY CHALLENGE®

*Have students discuss these questions:*

*Ask*

- **What would it take for you to turn to the Bible in your daily life more than you do now?**

- **How could you make Bible reading a more regular part of your schedule?**

- **What are your three biggest questions or concerns about the Bible?**

- **Who specifically could you go to when you have questions about what you read in the Bible?**

*Have everyone choose a Daily Challenge that they can keep to in the days that follow.*

*Ask*

- **What one thing will you commit to doing in order to rely on the Bible for every part of your life?**

*Have each student find a partner to pray with regarding their commitments. Before students leave, remind them to follow through on their Daily Challenge commitment—and to tell someone how it goes.*

## PARENT CONNECT

Distribute the "Family Life" devotional from the *Essential Messages* CD to students, and encourage them to complete the devotional with their families in the next several days.

# ③ Pick a Path, but Not Just Any Path

12|11|11

## TOPIC
**Choices**

## SCRIPTURE
■ Matthew 7:13-14

## PURPOSE
To help students commit to choices that will please God and bring them closer to Jesus.

## SUPPLIES NEEDED
■ *Essential Messages* CD
■ Bibles
■ Masking tape
■ Two different types of treats, such as Hershey's Kisses chocolates and lollipops (one treat for each student)
■ TV, VCR/DVD player, and *Bruce Almighty* video/DVD (Universal, 2003)
■ Dry-erase board and dry-erase marker or a sheet of newsprint and regular marker

## SET-UP
■ Set up the VCR/DVD player, and cue *Bruce Almighty* to 17:45 (if you're using a VCR, set the counter to 0:00:00 when the studio logo appears). Watch the clip at least once before students arrive.

■ Print enough "Pick-a-Path" handouts from the *Essential Messages* CD so that every three or four students has a copy.

■ Use masking tape to create a large Y on the floor of your meeting area.

■ Set up a dry-erase board or tape a sheet of newsprint to a wall in preparation for the activity in the "Pathway 2: The Narrow Road" section.

---

### TIP FOR THE LEADER

If you have a group of more than 20 teenagers, you may want to create more than one Y in order to save time and to enable better group discussions during this activity.

## Starting Off
### A Tale of Two Roads

*As teenagers arrive, have them line up at the stem of the Y you created with masking tape.*

To begin today, you have to make a choice about which path you'll choose. Will you follow the masking tape path to the right or to the left? I can't tell you what will happen when you get to the end of the path; the future is unclear. But everyone has to make a choice.

To emphasize the idea that what we value is shown by the choices we make in our search for meaning in life, show the clip (00:15:09 through 00:19:46) titled "I Still Haven't Found What I'm Looking For" from U2's *Rattle and Hum* video/DVD. (Be sure to preview the clip before using it.) Afterward, ask questions such as the following:

- What are the band members searching for? Where are they looking?

- Why do you think they still haven't found what they're looking for?

- What does their search reveal about what they value?

After each person has walked along the path of his or her choice, distribute two different kinds of treats—chocolate candy to the teenagers who chose one path and lollipops to teenagers who chose the other, for example. Have students form two seated groups—one group of those who chose the path to the right and one group of those who chose the path to the left—and discuss these questions:

*Ask*

- **Why did you choose the path you chose?**

- **How did you go about making the choice?**

There's a famous poem by Robert Frost that talks about two roads, and how taking the one less traveled "has made all the difference."

*Ask*

- **Why do you think the less-traveled path made such a difference?**

- **When have you experienced this in your own life?**

 - **When faced with a choice in your daily life, how do you go about making decisions?**

- **How do your priorities and values affect your decisions?**

When faced with a choice, people tend to make a decision based on their values and on what they think each choice will bring them. Fortunately for you, both choices today—the path to the right and the path to the left—led to a pretty good place. Today we're going to explore how the decisions we make take us on a journey down one path or another. The path we choose via those decisions will make all the difference in our lives.

# Digging In
## Only One Path Leads to Life

*Ask a volunteer to read aloud Matthew 7:13-14.*

 Just as you had to make a choice today about which masking-tape path to choose, everyone has this choice to make at some point in life: to follow the narrow road or the broad road. Jesus says one road leads to life, and one leads to destruction. The choice seems simple, doesn't it? It's a no-brainer! Then why do so many people choose the broad road, and why do only a few people find the narrow road? And how do the little decisions we make each day lead us toward one road or the other?

## Pathway 1: The Broad Road

Let's look at the first pathway, the one Jesus calls "broad." The following video clip shows an example of someone who is traveling the broad road. Take a look.

*Gather all the students together to view the clip from* Bruce Almighty. *Begin the clip at 0:17:45, and end the clip at 0:20:1. Then lead a short discussion.*

*Ask*

- **What motivates Bruce to make the decisions he makes?**

- **If Bruce continues making choices based on the same values or priorities, what do you think will be the results?**

- **Based on this example, how would you describe the broad road?**

On the broad road, we find people who are pursuing their own selfish desires, often without considering the consequences to others. They may believe that they'll find happiness, satisfaction, and total fulfillment if every decision they make takes them closer to satisfying those desires. However, there are some major flaws with deciding to chase after our selfish desires at any cost.

*Ask*

- **What do you believe are some of the major flaws in thinking that if we pursue our desires, we'll find happiness?**

Even if we consistently make choices that fulfill our every desire, we are focused on one thing—ourselves. The broad road looks good to a lot of people because it seems to lead to happiness and fulfilled desires. But at the end of the road, we may find that having our every desire fulfilled does not bring happiness. We may find that we are alone because of our selfishness. We may find that we can't deal with setbacks in life. We may find that with every desire we meet, a new one crops up. We may find that our lives look full on the outside but are truly empty on the inside.

*Ask*

- **Why do you think so many people choose the broad road?**

- **How can you know whether a particular decision will lead you down the broad road?**

- **Why do you think Jesus described this road as "broad"?**

*Ask several students to form two parallel lines as the "broad road." The two lines should be at least 10 feet apart from each other. As you speak, zigzag around within the space they've created.*

On the broad road, you can wander around without a clear direction or goal. When you have a choice to make, you have lots of room to make different decisions. *Turn to your right, keeping within the "road."* You might make a decision that takes you this direction. *Turn to your left, again keeping within the "road."* Or you might make a decision that takes you this direction. There is no one clear direction on the broad road. Anything goes. *Continue zigzagging within the "road."* And because this road is broad, many people find it and never search past it to find the narrow road.

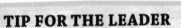

## TIP FOR THE LEADER

Teenagers may interpret this discussion about pursuing desires as a message that having and pursuing dreams and goals is wrong. It's not—in fact, it's great! But making choices to bring about those dreams no matter what and depending upon those dreams to bring ultimate fulfillment, meaning, and significance in life takes us down the broad path. Only a relationship with Jesus produces fulfillment and meaning. What's more, when we follow Jesus, he shapes our dreams in such a way that they will glorify him. In other words, he gives us high-value dreams that are worth pursuing.

# Pathway 2: The Narrow Road

Now let's take a closer look at the narrow road.

*Have the students in the parallel lines step closer together so that there is only about two feet of space between the lines.*

Once you've found the narrow road, you have focus and direction. When you have a choice to make, it's clear that you must make the decision that keeps you headed down the road. *To illustrate this, look to your right and left, and then walk toward the "end" of the "road." Then allow the students forming the lines to sit down.*

*Ask a volunteer to read aloud Matthew 7:13-14 again. Then lead a discussion.*

*Ask*

- **What does it mean that this is the road that leads to life?**

- **How do you think a person can find the narrow road?**

- **Why do you think only a few people find it?**

 *Have students form groups of three or four, and give each group a "Pick-a-Path" handout. Explain that groups are to compare the narrow road to the broad road and write down their answers. After about four minutes, draw two columns on the dry-erase board or newsprint. Above one column write "Broad Road"; above the other column write "Narrow Road." Ask each small group to share with the whole group one comparison they made. Write their comments in the columns. Then have groups discuss the following questions:*

*Ask*

- **Why do you think that even once people have discovered the narrow road, they choose not to travel it?**

- **How do choices and decisions impact our ability to find the narrow road? How does trying to stay on the narrow road impact the choices and decisions we make?**

- **What are some examples of choices that keep us from finding the narrow road?**

- **What are some examples of choices that *help us* find the narrow road?**

On the broad road, people generally are focused on fulfilling their own desires. On the narrow road, people are focused on Christ and doing what honors him. This means, above all, loving God and loving their neighbors. This is not the "anything goes" attitude that prevails on the broad road. On the narrow road, every choice is filtered through the question of how to demonstrate love for God and neighbor. If this sounds dreary and difficult, you now understand why so many people choose the broad road! But remember, Jesus says that a relationship with him is *exactly* what leads to life. Focusing on loving him and others builds the most fulfilling, most meaningful life possible.

# Wrapping Up

*Have everyone stand up and move to an area of your meeting space where there are no chairs or tables (an area where students can walk around easily). Have everyone in the group turn and face one wall; the group does not have to be organized in any particular manner as long as everyone is facing the same way. Then choose a few students—roughly 10 percent of the group—to turn and face a different wall. Explain that when you say go, everyone should walk toward the wall they're facing. Call out "Go!" After everyone has reached a wall, bring students back together to discuss these questions:*

*Ask*

- **For those of you who walked against the crowd, what was this experience like?**
- **For everyone else, what was this experience like?**
- **What additional insights about the broad path did you get from this experience?**
- **What insights about the narrow path did you get?**

The narrow path that Jesus challenges us to travel is not separated from the broad road; it's smack in the middle of the broad road. Traveling the narrow path takes consistent effort and conscientious decision making, but it's worth it because the choices we make in our everyday lives so affect our journey.

Are you consistently searching for the narrow road? Are your choices helping or hurting your search?

Bring in a rotten piece of wood, and have students paint it. Then have students discuss how believing that fulfilled desires brings about happiness and meaning is like painting a rotten piece of wood: The paint only changes the outside appearance of the wood but does not improve the rotten condition of the wood. The same is true with most desires: Fulfilling a desire might change a person's life on the outside but generally does not improve the inward condition of the person.

# DAILY CHALLENGE®

*Have students form groups of two or three to discuss these questions:*

*Ask*

- **What makes traveling the narrow road so difficult?**

- **Why do you think people choose the narrow road even though it's more challenging?**

- **Think about a choice looming in your life. What are some possible "broad-road" decisions you could make? What are some possible "narrow-road" decisions?**

*Have everyone choose a Daily Challenge that they'll follow through on in the days that follow.*

*Ask*

- **What one thing will you commit to doing this week to help others in our group find or travel the narrow road?**

*Close in prayer. Ask God to help your group create an atmosphere that champions narrow-road traveling. Before students leave, remind them to follow through on their Daily Challenge commitment—and to tell someone how it goes.*

# 4 Our Place in God's Space

## TOPIC
Community

## SCRIPTURE
- Acts 2
- Romans 16:3-15

## PURPOSE
To help students become essential parts of a community that's diverse, welcoming, faith-building, and centered on Jesus.

## SUPPLIES NEEDED
- *Essential Messages* CD
- Bibles
- Newsprint, masking tape, and a marker
- TV, VCR/DVD player, and *Keeping the Faith* video/DVD (Touchstone Pictures, 2000)
- Paper and pencils
- A ball of yarn for every 6 to 10 people

## SET-UP
- Print enough "TV Communities" handouts from the *Essential Messages* CD for every four students to have one.

- Print enough "Parent Connect: Mealtime" handouts from the *Essential Messages* CD for each student to have one.

- Set up the TV and VCR/DVD player, and cue *Keeping the Faith* to 00:10:37 (if you're using a VCR, set the counter to 0:00:00 when the studio logo appears). Preview the clip at least once before students arrive.

- Write this message's discussion questions on newsprint, but keep it hidden until the discussions.

## BONUS IDEA

For added authenticity and fun during this activity, wear a colored apron similar to those used at gourmet coffee shops.

## Starting Off
### Exploring Differences

I've noticed that just about everyone enjoys a tasty beverage from the coffee shop. But we all like different drinks. Just imagine I'm the person who takes your order at the coffee shop. On the count of three, shout out your order for your favorite hot drink. Ready? One, two, three!

There *is* a point to this. We might all participate in this group and be close to the same age—well, at least you all are—but we're very different, too. Have you ever wondered how we pull that off?

We're united in following Jesus. We just ordered our coffee drinks to show our differences, but now on the count of three, let's say "Jesus" to show our unity. One, two, three...Jesus!

Jesus unites us, even though we're different from each other.

Today we're going to explore this idea of being united in Christ as a community. One of the best biblical examples of unity despite differences can be found in the book of Acts, when people learned that Christian communities could be diverse but centered on Jesus.

# Digging In
## The Christian Church Began in Community

*Summarize Acts 2.*

Pentecost was an important, holy day for the people of Israel. Every year, people would come from all over the world to Jerusalem to worship and celebrate. They brought their different languages, cultures, and—I'm sure—different coffee drinks. Or, maybe not.

On the Pentecost after Jesus' death and resurrection, his disciples were also in Jerusalem to celebrate. Jesus had promised them that he'd send the Holy Spirit to guide them. And at Pentecost that year, God's Holy Spirit came.

What a scene! Let's hear how the Bible describes it.

*Invite an expressive reader to read aloud Acts 2:1-12.*

The Bible says that despite all the differences among the people who were present that Pentecost, "about three thousand were added to their number that day" (Acts 2:41). What happened when the church came into being several centuries ago applies to us today. Because of Jesus, all of us—as different as we are—come together as one.

## Jesus Brings People Together

*Direct teenagers to form pairs with someone they don't know very well. While students form pairs, tape up the sheet of newsprint with the discussion questions below on it.*

*Once everyone has found a partner, have pairs first find something they don't have in common. Then have pairs discuss the questions below:*

*Ask*

- **What are some differences among people in this group?**

- **In what specific ways are we united by Jesus?**

- **What can we do to grow closer to Jesus together, despite our differences?**

## Communities Are Welcoming

Community is difficult. That's true in our group just as in any other community. Even though the church began as a united community, differences began to divide it. Let's take a look at the early church in Acts, see how it compares to other communities you're familiar with, and see what we can learn about the community of the church.

 *Have each pair find another pair to make a group of four. Distribute a Bible, a "TV Communities" handout from the* Essential Messages *CD, and a pencil to each group. Give groups five to 10 minutes to work. Then ask several groups to share with everyone what they discussed.*

One important characteristic of the early church was that they welcomed everyone. How well do you think our group is doing at welcoming everyone?

*Pause for a few moments for students to shout out a few responses.*

True community that's focused on Jesus welcomes everyone and doesn't exclude anyone. The opposite of community is a clique, which is small, exclusive, and nonwelcoming.

*Read aloud Acts 2:46-47.*

The early church was welcoming and attractive to outsiders. It was the kind of community that others wanted to join, and the people in the church were delighted to welcome them.

*Ask*

- **What are some specific things our group needs to do to welcome everyone and not exclude people?**

## Faith Communities Help Us Grow Closer to Jesus

Vibrant communities don't just feel welcoming. They also help us to grow in our relationship with Jesus. We're going to watch a movie clip about two best friends who grew up together. One became a rabbi, and the other became a priest. In this scene, each man is developing as a leader of a faith community. Watch how these communities reflect what we've been talking about so far, and watch how these communities are growing together.

*Play the clip of* Keeping the Faith, *beginning at 00:10:37 and ending at 00:13:40 after the priest says, "Let us pray."*

*Have teenagers get into new groups of four to discuss these questions. As they're forming groups, tape to a wall the sheet of newsprint with the discussion questions below written on it. Each group also will need a Bible.*

### TIP FOR THE LEADER

Teenagers relate to the communities they see on-screen, even wanting to be a part of their favorite TV show's circle of friends. Sadly, TV shows may provide the only examples of community some of our teenagers see. Help them look beyond the ideas of community presented in these shows to the real community Jesus desires for us as his people.

### BONUS IDEA

Expand the discussion on your group's hospitality. Ask questions such as, "How do we welcome new people who visit our group?" "What sort of follow-up do we do with first-time visitors?" "Who might feel out of place if they came here, and how could we help them to feel more at home?" and "What can we do to invite more people to join us?"

*Ask*

- **What most stood out to you about the sense of community portrayed?**
- **How were these communities growing together and worshipping God?**
- **How were these communities similar to and different from the faith community you read about in Acts?**

In the movie we saw how the leaders of the synagogue and the church helped people grow closer to God. They also grew because they interacted with one another. An early leader in the church, Paul, wrote that many different people were helping the Christian churches of the time.

*In each group, have a student read aloud Romans 16:3-15.*

I'm sure Paul could have told us all the different kinds of coffee drinks these people liked, too! Seriously, though, we don't know who many of these people were. But they helped to welcome other people to know Jesus, and they all grew closer to Jesus together. The same happens with us today. Let's explore how that happens.

*Distribute a sheet of paper and a pencil to each person.*

At the top of your paper, write "Past." Then write the names of three people in your past who helped you to learn about Jesus.

*Provide time for students to work.*

Now at the middle of your paper, write "Present." Write the names of three people who help you these days to follow Jesus.

*Give students time to discuss.*

Now toward the bottom of your paper, write "Future." Write the names or titles of people in your future whom you'll rely on to help you follow Jesus. It could be a college professor, boss, spouse, or even children you could have.

*Give students time to work.*

Turn to a partner and briefly share what you wrote and why.

*Give students time to share.*

The Christian community can help us to grow. It's been that way since Pentecost. Yes, sometimes we don't do so well. Yes, we have some room to grow. But this group has an impact on you, and *you* have an impact on others in this group. God is using you.

# Wrapping Up

*Have teenagers form groups of six to 10 based on something they have in common with one another, and have each group form a circle. Give each group a ball of yarn.*

When it's time, throw the ball of yarn to someone across the circle and say something you appreciate about that person or how that person makes our community better. The person who throws the ball of yarn needs to hold on to the end of it. Then the person who catches the ball of yarn holds the yarn and throws the ball to someone else and affirms him or her. Keep doing this, holding the string of yarn as you catch it and throw it to someone else. We'll do this for four minutes, and you'll see a web developing in your circles. People can receive the yarn more than once, but make sure each person receives it at least once. Go!

*After four minutes, call time. Instruct the oldest and youngest members of each group to drop the yarn, then the person wearing the most blue. Have groups discuss these questions.*

*Ask*

- **How does dropping the yarn affect the group?**

- **How is that like what happens when we're not an active part of the community?**

*Invite the people who dropped the yarn to pick it up again, making the web tight once more. Have everyone join in prayer, thanking God for this community of faith that helps us grow closer to Jesus.*

## PARENT CONNECT

Distribute the "Parent Connect: Mealtimes" handout from the *Essential Messages* CD to teenagers before they leave so they can do the activities with their families.

This message could coincide with Pentecost to help students understand the beginning of the church. Since Pentecost is the church's birthday, celebrate with birthday cake, balloons, and singing "Happy Birthday."

You also could use this message in conjunction with learning about your church's or denomination's history. Invite your pastor or other church leader to talk with your students about your church's past, present, and future sense of community.

Group Publishing has a number of resources designed to develop community in your youth group. See *Friendship: Creating a Culture of Connectivity in Your Church* (Group, 2005) and *Friendship First: Youth Ministry Kit* (Group, 2005). Go to www.group.com.

# DAILY CHALLENGE®

*Have students form pairs. Challenge teenagers to commit to supporting their faith community in one specific way during the coming week and to share that commitment with their partners. If they need ideas, suggest praying for the group, inviting someone to be a part of the community, or intentionally getting to know someone in the community better.*

*Before students leave, remind them to follow through on their Daily Challenge commitment—and to tell their partners how it goes.*

# ⑤ Welcome to Church— Let's Fight!

## TOPIC

Conflict

## SCRIPTURE

- Proverbs 27:17
- Matthew 5:21-26; 15:1-11
- Acts 15:1-19

## PURPOSE

To help students explore practical, Christ-like ways they can deal with conflict.

## SUPPLIES NEEDED

- *Essential Messages* CD
- CD player
- Bibles
- Newsprint, masking tape, and a marker
- Blocks of unsanded wood and pieces of sandpaper (one of each per student)
- Newspapers and news magazines

## SET-UP

- Set up the CD player with the *Essential Messages* CD cued to track 3, "A Conversation in Two Rounds."

**BONUS IDEA**

Bring in a labor-dispute mediator or human-resources manager to talk about conflict resolution in the secular or professional world.

## Starting Off

Some people love conflict, and some people love to avoid it. Let's see how well *we* deal with conflict.

### Responding to Conflict

I need a volunteer who can talk for a while about something you love. It should be something about which you can speak really enthusiastically, whether pizza, a friend, a sport, a hobby, or whatever. I'll warn you ahead of time that everyone else is invited to disagree with you, and you must respond to every question or challenge you get.

*Have the volunteer stand up in front of the room to give a short speech.*

You all are free to give comments or ask questions, but you can't yell over the speaker so that we can't hear him or her. We want to see some common ways people respond to conflict, so your job is to be the conflict!

*Allow the volunteer to speak, and encourage interaction from other teenagers. After several minutes, lead a short discussion.*

If you have a group of more than 16 teenagers, have them form groups of 8 to 10 and complete this activity in those smaller groups. As groups work, be sure to circulate to keep groups on track and ensure that they understand what to do.

Also, closely moderate the discussions. The goal is to create an energetic example of how complicated conflict can feel, not to be rude or hurtful.

• *(To the speaker)* **What does it feel like to have people challenge you like this?**

• *(To the rest of the group)* **What is it like to challenge someone?**

• **Do you find conflict stressful or exciting? Why?**

Conflict is inevitable in every relationship. However, there are better and worse ways to carry on a conflict. Jesus knows that we're going to conflict with one another, and today we're going to look at the ways he might want us to handle it.

# Digging In

*Distribute pieces of rough wood and sandpaper. As the students listen to the CD track below and discuss it, have them sand down a piece of wood.*

## Conflict Is Normal

Listen to these two conversations between a mother and daughter, and think about why the two versions conclude differently. Be prepared to discuss what each person says that might anger the other and what each could say to better address the conflict.

*Play track 3, "A Conversation in Two Rounds," from the* Essential Messages *CD.*

*As students listen, tape a sheet of newsprint to a wall. After the track has finished, turn off the CD player.*

*Ask teenagers to call out words and phrases from these conversations that may have stirred anger, and write their ideas on the sheet of newsprint. Then ask the group to call out skills, characteristics, words, and phrases people can use in similar situations to better deal with a conflict.*

*Afterward, lead a discussion.*

*Ask*

• **Why did these conversations go differently?**

• **How might these conversations have been different if the mother and daughter had been thinking about what Jesus would do?**

• **What helps us steer away from hurtful conflict and toward resolution?**

*Ask a volunteer to read aloud Matthew 15:1-11.*

Conflict was a normal part of Jesus' life, too, just as it's a normal part of our lives. The Pharisees challenged him frequently, and often Jesus responded to those challenges and actually used them to teach the crowd. So when it comes to conflict, the idea is not to avoid it at all costs. If we try to avoid it, it will find us anyway. The idea is to approach the conflict in the most loving way possible—more like the second conversation we heard on the CD. When we approach conflict with love and understanding for the person with whom we're in conflict, we may even learn something from the situation.

## Conflict Can Be Healthy

*Read aloud Proverbs 27:17.*

*Ask*

- **How does the piece of wood you've been sanding reflect the message of this proverb?**
- **How might conflict help us learn and mature?**
- **In the CD conversations between the mother and daughter, how might this mother and daughter have been sharpening one another?**
- **What might be the results of this kind of sharpening?**

*Have teenagers each turn to a partner to discuss the following.*

*Ask*

- **Describe a time when you experienced a similar sharpening in your own life.**
- **Are there certain elements in your life about which you always find yourself in conflict? If so, what are they?**

Discuss together how conflict might help polish your character over time just as you polished the piece of wood.

*Have students form groups of about four. Explain that their task is to come to a resolution on a topic you assign them. Topics should include something on which your students might have a wide variety of opinions, though you might want to avoid heated social issues. For example, you could assign groups topics such as "downloading free music," "city-wide curfews for teens," and "lower age limits for R-rated movies."*

*Allow five minutes for all the group members to discuss and come to an agreement regarding their position on the topic. Encourage teenagers to consult the words, phrases, and characteristics listed on the newsprint from the previous discussion as they attempt to come to resolution. Then have each group join with another group of four and try to come to an agreement within the new group of eight. Allow another five minutes for this. Afterward, lead a discussion.*

*Ask*

- **What was it like to come to an agreement with a group of four? with a group of eight?**
- **What makes it difficult for everyone to agree?**

Encourage your teenagers to think about a conflict they have had recently with their parents. Ask youth to create a list of three possible compromises they might offer to their parents to resolve the conflict. Urge students to approach their parents this week and ask them about conflict in the family, perhaps with a general question such as "Why do families tend to have conflict?" Through the conversation, teenagers can identify the contentious issue and help to bring it to resolution with their compromises.

• **How are our interactions different when we keep Jesus and his teachings at the forefront of our conversations?**

In your groups, read Acts 15:1-19.

In the first few centuries of the church, when great conflicts arose, the church resolved them by gathering together top leaders to discuss the issues and come to resolution. Without conflict, they wouldn't have become unified over these discussions and subjects.

*Have groups discuss these questions:*

*Ask*

• **Why might we need some conflict in our lives?**

• **In addition to polishing our character, how does conflict help us?**

• **What may have happened in the very early church if the leaders had simply avoided the conflict over circumcision that's described in Acts 15?**

All of us have rough edges, which is why conflict always will exist between people. But conflict can be a healthy part of our growth as God uses it to sand down and polish our character, refining us into what we are supposed to be. So rather than simply trying to avoid all disagreements, we might want to see them as unique opportunities for God to steer us in new directions. Through conflict, we may learn creative ideas and new insights from the people with whom we disagree.

## Resolution Requires Love and Grace

*Distribute a newspaper or news magazine to each small group. In their groups, have students identify a conflict in the world and then discuss what sacrifices both sides of the conflict would have to make in order to achieve resolution. Have groups discuss these questions:*

*Ask*

• **What would you do if you were personally involved in this conflict?**

• **In situations like this one, what ideas or attitudes make it easy to remain in conflict with others or even to escalate the conflict?**

• **If both sides of this conflict decided to commit to Jesus' values, how might the conflict be different?**

• **What would it take for this conflict to be resolved?**

In your group, take a minute to pray for resolution to a particular world conflict that touches your hearts.

*Have a volunteer read aloud Matthew 5:21-26.*

Conflicts often escalate when we stop seeing the person we disagree with as a child of God and start seeing that person as a stereotype, as a name such as "Raca" or "you fool," or as a threat. If we don't see a person as a child of God, it removes our responsibility to treat that person as such. To come to resolution, we have to meet the person—go directly to him or her as the Scripture indicates—so we can see the person once again as a brother or sister. Then we have to be willing to settle matters, even if it means giving up some of our own desires. Basically, we have to extend the same love and grace to others as God extends to us.

Peace in world conflicts would require a lot of people to follow these simple teachings of Jesus. As impossible as this might seem, such peace begins with each one of us living out Jesus' teachings in our own lives.

# Wrapping Up

Conflict is a normal part of relationships. It can actually help us to grow into mature followers of Christ as he sands down our rough edges. As we take Jesus' view on the issues that bring us into conflict, we tend to put aside our own needs to honor other people.

## PARENT CONNECT

If someone in your church specializes in conflict mediation, ask that person to teach a workshop to your teenagers' parents. Through the workshop, parents could learn some effective techniques for dealing with the conflicts that seem to arise on a daily basis during their kids' teenage years.

# DAILY CHALLENGE®

*Have students discuss the following questions:*

*Ask*

- **What are the most common sources of conflict in your life?**

- **Have you ever thought of those conflicts as gifts from God to help sand down some of your rough edges?**

- **What might be a rough edge in your life that God is trying to sand down right now?**

*Have everyone choose a Daily Challenge they'll follow through on in the days that follow.*

*Ask*

- **What one thing will you commit to doing to address a conflict in which you're currently involved? For instance, is there an apology you need to make? Is there someone you need to spend more time listening to?**

*Have everyone turn to a friend and share their commitment.*

*Before students leave, remind them to follow through on their Daily Challenge commitment—and to tell someone how it goes.*

# 6 Doubting Thomas, Doubting (Your Name Here)

## TOPIC
**Doubt**

## SCRIPTURE
■ John 20:24-31

## PURPOSE
To encourage students to be honest about their doubts with God, who strengthens their faith and trust.

## SUPPLIES NEEDED
■ *Essential Messages* CD
■ Bible
■ Paper and pens
■ At least one wide-mouth container for every four students
■ Dried beans
■ Table-tennis balls
■ Resealable plastic bags

## SET-UP
■ Print enough copies of the "True-False Quiz" from the *Essential Messages* CD for every student to have one.

■ Gather one wide-mouth container for every four students. Depending on the size of your containers, put one to three table-tennis balls in first, and then fill it with dried beans. Shake the container gently so the beans settle, and then fill the container with a few more beans so that it's entirely full. (See Leader Tip on p. 41.) Place the table-tennis balls and beans into a resealable plastic bag and seal the bag.

---

### BONUS IDEA

Give students an index card and pen, and ask them to write an anonymous statement reflecting a doubt about God, Christianity, the Bible and so forth. Collect the cards and randomly select one to read, allowing others who have doubted and come to conviction on that issue to share their journeys.

## Starting Off

Let's take a quick true-false quiz that I'm sure will raise a few doubts in your minds.

*Distribute a pen and "True-False Quiz" from the Essential Messages CD to each person, and allow three to five minutes for students to buzz through the quiz. Then go over the answers (provided in the box in the margin) and lead a short discussion.*

**TIP FOR THE LEADER**

Some quiet background music may help your students tune out distractions and concentrate on being honest with God.

**TIP FOR THE LEADER**

Some students in your group likely have the spiritual gift of faith, which makes it easier for them to believe. They may react to this topic with skepticism, doubting that others really struggle with doubt. Help them see their gift for what it is—a gift and an opportunity to be used by God to encourage others to believe.

*Ask*

- **How did you decide what was true and what was false? Explain.**

- **In life, how do you decide what is true?**

- **How do you feel when you doubt something?**

*Ask students to form groups of four and come up with a top-five list of things teenagers doubt—for example, family stability, popularity, intelligence, or the future. After two to three minutes, ask groups to share their lists. If no one mentions God's existence, miracles, the Bible's veracity, or other faith issues, help them get there.*

## Everyone Doubts

Everyone doubts. It's natural. Sometimes your doubts come from simple intellectual curiosity such as "Who created the Nobel Prizes and why?" Other times, your doubts will be intensely personal, such as whether your parents' marriage will survive this latest blowup. And at some point in life, almost everyone has doubts of a spiritual nature. We all have questions that need answers or, if no answers can be had, an experience of God (or both!).

Since everyone doubts, doubting doesn't make you a bad person or a bad Christian. It's what you do with your doubts that matters. Let's talk more about that now.

# Digging In
## God Can Meet You in Your Doubt

*Read aloud John 20:24-31.*

Thomas doubted, and no lightning bolt from heaven came to strike him down. Instead, Jesus showed up and was gentle with him. Thomas' honesty about his doubts became an opportunity for God to work.

*Provide paper and pens for teenagers to write God an honest letter about their own doubts, including their feelings about being honest with God about their doubts and how they would like God to meet them in their doubts. After several minutes, lead a discussion.*

*Ask*

- **How did it feel to bring your doubt to God?**

- **How do you expect God to respond to your doubt?**

- **Do you think God's feelings for you will change because of your doubt? Why or why not?**

Thomas lived and worked with Jesus for the three years of Jesus' earthly ministry. He heard Jesus predict his own death and resurrection, and yet Thomas doubted that Jesus' predictions had come true—despite the other disciples' eyewitness accounts—until he could see it for himself. Jesus loved Thomas enough to give him what he needed in order to believe, and Jesus will respond to you and your doubts with the same love and gentleness he showed to Thomas.

## God Can Help You Stop Doubting and Believe

Thomas believed because he saw; when we believe without seeing, Jesus says we are blessed for it. The gospel accounts have been recorded for us so that we can believe even though we may not see with our physical eyes.

*Have students form groups of four. Give each group a wide-mouth container, beans, and table-tennis balls. Ask them to put the beans and balls in their containers so that everything fits. Unless they've seen this object lesson before, students likely will doubt that everything will fit in the container. Allow them to struggle for a few minutes before showing them how it works: If you put the beans in first, the balls won't fit; but if you put the balls in first, everything will fit. Afterward, lead a discussion.*

*Ask*

- **How did you feel trying to get all the beans and balls into the container? Explain.**

- **Did you believe it could be done? Why or why not?**

Believe it or not, this activity is like the doubts in our lives. If we put all our doubts, concerns, fears, and so on into our lives first, we will crowd out any room for belief. But if we allow room for God by filling ourselves with things like Scripture—with accounts of real people like us who lived, doubted, and believed—then the doubts can be seen for what they are: small stuff next to the important matters of life.

## Wrapping Up

Everyone doubts. God wants to meet you in your doubt and help you to believe. As you bring your doubts to our loving God, you may not get immediate answers. But your relationship with Jesus will grow as you trust him to walk with you in your doubts.

---

## PARENT CONNECT

Many parents doubt their ability to connect with their teenagers, especially on matters of faith, and count on you to do that for them. Giving parents the scoop on what you are teaching each week or each month can help them know at least where to begin a conversation about what their teenagers are learning. If you send out a monthly newsletter, include the key point, key Scripture, and one follow-up question parents can ask their teens for each lesson you'll teach that month. It takes some advance preparation on your part, but it will go far to helping parents and teenagers relate. They'll thank you for it!

# DAILY CHALLENGE®

*Tell students to take one bean from their container. Lead them in a short prayer in which they "name" their bean with their doubts. Ask students to mentally give God their doubts then commit to a Daily Challenge that will help them do something with their doubts. For example, they could write down their doubts and put them in their Bibles to pray about, or talk about their doubts with a Christian friend.*

*Ask*

- **What one thing will you commit to doing with your doubts this week that will help you grow in your trust for God?**

*Teenagers can take the bean with them to help them remember their Daily Challenge. Before students leave, remind them to follow through on their Daily Challenge commitment—and to tell someone how it goes.*

# Families: You Can't Live With 'Em, You Can't Live Without 'Em

*1|8|12*

## TOPIC
**Family**

## SCRIPTURE
- Genesis 25:26-34; 27:1–28:5; 37:2-36
- Matthew 20:20-24
- Ephesians 6:1-3
- Colossians 3:20

## PURPOSE
To help students understand the importance of honoring and loving their families even when it's really, really tough.

## SUPPLIES NEEDED
- *Essential Messages* CD
- CD player
- Bibles
- TV, VCR/DVD player, and *My Big Fat Greek Wedding* video/DVD (Gold Circle Films/HBO Video, 2002)
- Index cards
- Paper and pens
- U2 *How to Dismantle an Atomic Bomb* CD

## SET-UP
- Set up the TV and VCR/DVD player with *My Big Fat Greek Wedding* cued to approximately 0:03:45 (if you're using a VCR, set the counter to 0:00:00 when the studio logo appears). Preview the clip at least once before students arrive.

- Set up the CD player with the *How to Dismantle an Atomic Bomb* CD ready to play the song "Sometimes You Can't Make it on Your Own," (track 3).

- Print a "Love and Honor" handout from the *Essential Messages* CD for each student.

## Starting Off
### It Can Be Tough to Get Along With Our Families

*To illustrate that it can be tough to get along with our families, show a clip from* My Big Fat Greek Wedding. *If you're using a VCR, set the counter to 0:00:00 when the studio logo appears. Begin the clip at approximately 0:03:45 when Toula's mother opens the oven. End the clip at approximately 0:06:25 when Toula turns to walk into her school.*

Can you relate to Toula? We all feel annoyed, embarrassed, or irritated by our families from time to time. Take a moment to silently think of a recent experience that caused you to feel really annoyed, embarrassed, or irritated with a family member.

## TIP FOR THE LEADER

If students need help, share an example such as the following scenario:

My dad called my soccer coach to complain that I wasn't playing. I was really embarrassed, and I feel like my coach is annoyed at me now.

*Distribute index cards and pens.*

Once you've thought of an experience, write a short description of the incident on the card I gave you. There's one important rule: Don't include any names. Write it in such a way that people won't know who wrote it or that it is about your family.

*Allow teenagers a few minutes to write, and then collect all the cards and shuffle them. Have teenagers form groups of four; then distribute four of the index cards to each small group. Explain that you'd like small groups to read all four cards then decide together on one card that they find to be the most annoying, irritating, or embarrassing. Have a volunteer from each small group read aloud their selected card to the larger group.*

Wow! Those were some really excruciating experiences! It's not always easy to get along with our families, especially during the teenage years.

*Collect all the index cards for use later in the message. Then have small groups discuss the following questions:*

*Ask*

- **How has your relationship with your family changed since you've been a teenager? Have you experienced more conflict? Explain.**

- **What are the main causes of conflict you have with your family members?**

- **One common cause of family conflict is that teenagers view themselves as young adults while their family members view them as old children. Have you experienced this? If so, how has it made you feel?**

- **Why is it so hard to have positive communication with family members during your teenage years?**

- **Do you find it difficult to express positive emotions such as love, forgiveness, or friendship toward your family members? Do they seem to have a difficult time expressing those emotions toward you? Explain.**

There are lots of reasons why it can be really tough to get along with our families. But no matter how difficult it is, we should try.

# Digging In

Let's check out what the Bible has to say about how we relate to our families.

*Invite volunteers to read aloud Ephesians 6:1-3 and Colossians 3:20.*

Notice that the Bible doesn't say, "Honor your father and mother when they aren't getting on your nerves" or "Love your family *sometimes*." These verses, and many others in the Bible, teach us that we're to love and honor our families *all the time*. There are no ifs, ands, or buts about it. God knows it isn't always easy! In fact, Scripture is full of accounts of dysfunctional families just like yours! Even when it's really tough, we're to love our families...no matter what.

## Love Your Family, Even When Your Siblings Drive You Crazy

If you think your brother or sister is out to ruin your life, imagine how Esau must have felt.

*Summarize Genesis 25:26-34.*

So here's Esau, starving from a day of hunting, and his twin brother cons him into giving up his birthright—his place of honor in the family as the firstborn son. That's a high price for a bowl of stew! Clearly this negatively affected the relationship between the twin brothers.

*Summarize Genesis 27:1–28:5.*

As if things weren't bad enough, now Jacob acts like even more of a rat. He steals Esau's blessing! Jacob tricks his poor, old, blind dad into giving him a special blessing reserved for the older son, Esau. (Yes, they were twins, but Esau was born first.)

Jacob's treachery is the last straw—he knows he has offended his brother in the deepest way. And this isn't exactly what you want to do to a buff, hairy guy who excels in hunting! So what does Jacob do? He runs for his life.

Birthrights and blessings aren't really parts of our culture, so it may seem difficult at first to relate to this story. But have you ever been irritated at a sibling who took something that was yours? Or who tricked your parents and got away with something? Or who got a privilege that you don't have? Or what about Jacob's arrogance toward his brother? Have you ever felt like a sibling was prideful, self-centered, or rude? Jacob was his mother's favorite. Have you ever felt like a parent was playing favorites or that your sibling was getting spoiled?

Here's the thing: God knows your brothers and sisters get on your nerves sometimes. He's seen it all, from Jacob and Esau's conflicts to the fight you had with your sister last night. The Bible acknowledges that sibling relationships can get pretty dicey, but God calls you to step up to the plate anyway. You're to show love and honor to your brothers and sisters no matter what they may do to you. No excuses allowed.

## Love Your Family, Even if Your Parents Are Overbearing

Do you ever wish your parents would mind their own business and leave you alone? Do you feel like they're always asking, "Where are you

Help teenagers and their families have fun together! Revamp an upcoming youth meeting into a family night for teenagers, their parents, and their siblings. Plan games, creative activities, and snacks. Invite teenagers to prepare and present a short devotion for the night, focusing on how much they love and appreciate their families. This event will be a blessing to parents and a fun memory for teenagers and their siblings.

going? Who will you be with? When will you be home?" Are you longing for the day you graduate from high school and can be on your own and get your parents off your back?

If so, maybe you can relate to James and John, whose mother was still really nosy even when they were full-grown men.

*Invite a volunteer to read aloud Matthew 20:20-24.*

Can't you just picture it? James and John are hanging out with Jesus and the other disciples, when their loving mother shows up. What does she do? She has the nerve to ask Jesus if her sons can sit next to Jesus' throne in heaven! Scripture doesn't tell us if the boys put her up to it or not, but one thing we can see clearly from this passage: The other disciples were *not* happy about the request of James and John's mom.

Like many mothers, James and John's mom just wanted the best for her kids. Her intentions were good, but her behavior was inappropriate.

There may be lots of ways you feel your parents are overbearing. They might have strict rules about curfews or dating, they might be nosy about your phone conversations or e-mail, they might nag you constantly about homework and grades, they may set rules that drive you crazy. Or perhaps your parents do or say things that embarrass you in front of your friends. Or they might just really get on your nerves with their cheesy jokes, hokey hairdos, or inability to remember your friends' names.

God created families, so he knows all about the inevitable conflicts between parents and teenagers. God knows that it's tough to navigate this phase of life as you become more independent from your parents. But no matter how overbearing your parents are, you need to show them love and honor.

## Love Your Family, Even if It's a Nightmare

Here's one family in the Bible that's a certifiable disaster.

*Summarize Genesis 37:2-36.*

I'm sure glad I'm not a member of *this* family. We're not just talking about the typical conflict with parents and siblings. We're talking about really serious stuff. Jacob's favoritism toward his son Joseph must've really hurt his other sons' feelings. Joseph's dreams about his brothers submitting to him only added fuel to the fire. Then things really deteriorated: The brothers hated Joseph so much that they literally wanted to murder him. Instead, they stripped off his clothes, threw him into a pit, and then sold him to strangers as a slave. That's what I call serious abuse!

All of us deal with family strife: arguments, frustrations, or sibling rivalries. These are "normal" parts of growing up. But some of us may be living in a nightmare. We may come from a family situation that is full of hurt or pain. We may have been verbally or physically abused by a parent or a sibling. We may have been abandoned by a parent. We may have a family member who threatens us. We may feel completely ignored and unloved by parents who are too preoccupied to deal with us.

God sees your pain. God knows what you're going through. God can still use you in amazing ways, despite your bad family situation. Look at Joseph! Even though he had to go through so much terrible stuff as a young man, he ended up being Pharaoh's right-hand man. Not only was Joseph a leader of a nation, but he was also a *good person*. He wasn't "ruined for life" because of what his family did to him. Sure, it probably still hurt, but eventually he was able to move forward. He even forgave his brothers for the horrible things they did to him.

If you're like Joseph, if you're in a family situation that's a nightmare, turn to God for help. Be honest with God about your feelings—he cares for you! Ask God to help you show love and honor to your family members even when they do you wrong. This doesn't mean you have to *feel* loving toward the people who hurt you, and it doesn't mean you have to hide their abuse from others and just keep it to yourself. It means that you choose to be a loving and honorable person as you deal with the tough situation you're in. It means that, like Joseph, you won't let terrible circumstances turn you into someone who says or does cruel things to others.

If you're in one of those bad situations, don't only turn to God for help. Turn to other people, too. Please talk to me or another adult leader about the situation you're facing. We can help you—you don't have to go through this alone.

*Have students re-form their small groups of four (from the "Starting Off" activity), and lead them in discussion about their families and the challenges they face.*

*Ask*

- **Which of the three Bible stories do you relate to most? Why?**

- **Finish this sentence: It is hardest for me to love and honor my family when...**

- **Dream for a minute. What do you wish your relationships with your parents or siblings were like?**

- **What can you do to make that dream become a reality for your family?**

*While small groups are discussing these questions, shuffle the index cards again. Distribute four cards to each small group.*

It's easy to talk about showing love and honor to our families, but it can be hard to actually do it when the rubber meets the road. What does love in action look like? Read through the four situations on your cards, and discuss what a teenager could do to show love and honor to his or her family in each of these situations. And here's the rule: You can't be cheesy. Try to come up with words or actions that a teenager like you would actually *do*.

*Allow a few minutes for groups to come up with ideas; then explain that they should select one of the scenarios they discussed and*

## TIP FOR THE LEADER

If a student talks to you about serious problems in his or her family, consider referring the student (and the family) to a licensed Christian counselor. If a teenager reports a situation involving physical or sexual abuse, immediately contact your pastor and local authorities. You have a legal and ethical obligation to get that student out of a dangerous situation.

quickly prepare a 30-second skit that demonstrates the situation and a teenager's loving response. Have groups present their miniskits, and applaud their efforts.

Excellent job putting spiritual principles into practical actions. It isn't always easy to love and honor our families, but we need to do it no matter what.

# Wrapping Up

When we're constantly facing conflicts or irritation, it can be easy to forget how special our parents or siblings are to us. Sometimes we just plain take them for granted. The truth is that we never know how long we'll have our family members. We need to show them love and appreciation every day we have them in our lives.

I'd like to play a song for you that describes the conflict and misunderstandings that can happen between parents and children. This song was written by Bono of U2 about his dad. It explores not only the tough parts of a parent-child relationship but also the special bond that exists in families. This song was played at the funeral for Bono's dad.

As you listen to the words of this song, close your eyes and think about your own family. Do you take them for granted? What challenges do you face in getting along with them? How can you love them better?

*Play the song "Sometimes You Can't Make it On Your Own." When the song ends, ask teenagers to keep their eyes closed and silently pray, asking God to help them love and honor their families.*

*Wrap up the prayer time, and then direct small groups of four to gather together one more time.*

When we think about the possibility of losing our family members, we are reminded of how important it is to love and honor them every day. Let's celebrate the things we love about our families.

*Instruct students each to share with their small group one specific thing they appreciate about their parents or caregivers and one thing they appreciate about their siblings. (If teenagers don't have brothers or sisters, they can share two things they appreciate about their caregivers.)*

Even though they don't often show it, teenagers long to hear words of love and affirmation from their parents. Two weeks before the meeting, make arrangements for a parent of each student (or a grandparent or older sibling) to write a short letter of love and encouragement to their teenager. Have them submit the letters to you one week before the meeting.

If someone forgets, call to remind them. If some teenagers don't have family members who are willing to write a letter of encouragement (or if someone forgets), use the week prior to your meeting to make arrangements with other adults in the church family. Ask them to write encouraging notes, saying something like, "We may not be in the same biological family, but I'm glad you're part of my spiritual family!"

Give the letters to the teenagers at the end of the message.

# DAILY CHALLENGE®

 *Distribute paper and pens to small groups, and direct them to brainstorm and write down three very specific ways they can show love and honor to their family members. When they're done, distribute a "Love and Honor" handout from the* Essential Messages *CD to each student.*

Each group thought of three ways to show love and honor. Well, guess what: I expect you to do them! For the next month, let's commit to love and honor our families each day by completing a Daily Challenge. The "Love and Honor" handout contains a month's worth of life-application steps you can take to translate into action your commitment to love and honor your families. And see those three blank spots at the beginning? That's for you to write in the three specific ideas your group thought of.

*Allow a minute for teenagers to fill in the blanks on their handouts. Then close in prayer, asking God to help students show love and honor to their families even when it's really tough. Pray also for their efforts to live out the Daily Challenge suggestions each day for the next month.*

*Before students leave, remind them to follow through on their Daily Challenge commitments—and to tell someone how it goes. Also invite youth who are facing really hard situations in their families to take some time to talk with you about it.*

# ⑧ Onward Through the Storm

**TOPIC**

**Following Jesus**

**SCRIPTURE**

■ Matthew 14:1-33

**PURPOSE**

To help students follow Jesus even in the midst of life's toughest challenges.

**SUPPLIES NEEDED**

■ *Essential Messages* CD
■ CD player
■ Bible

**SET-UP**

■ Set up the CD player with the *Essential Messages* CD cued to track 4, "Sunny and Stormy."

---

**BONUS IDEA**

Find a clip from a stormy movie such as *The Perfect Storm* or *Twister,* or record a short segment on storms from the Weather Channel to use as a visual aid during this opening.

## Starting Off

Let's see who has the best storm story!

### Stormy Weather

*Have teenagers form groups of three or four. Ask each group member to share about the worst storm they've ever experienced. Then have several volunteers share someone else's story with the larger group.*

Crazy, intense, out-of-control storms—what a picture of life! Traveling through life can be like taking a walk when the sun is bright, the air is crisp, and there's not a cloud in the sky. Then...boom! Out of nowhere, a tornado appears. Perhaps you have a fight with your parents or a friend stabs you in the back or a loved one dies unexpectedly. No more sunny, crisp, fresh sky. Everything feels overcast and chaotic. Life goes from sunny to stormy. So how, in times of stormy chaos and confusion, does a person live out the Christian faith?

Use study guides such as commentaries on Matthew to help your teenagers more deeply understand the expectations Jews like Peter had for the Messiah. Help students see that part of Peter's "storm" came from his expectations of how life with a conquering Messiah was supposed to turn out. Lead teenagers in thinking through how their own inaccurate expectations contribute to stormy weather in their lives.

# Digging In
## A Real Storm Sprinter

*Summarize Matthew 14:1-21.*

In order to get into the mind of Jesus' disciple Peter, let's review a particularly stormy segment of his life. First, Jesus' cousin and friend, whom we know as John the Baptist, had been brutally murdered. More specifically, his head was severed from his body. This horrifying incident had to have caused swirling storm clouds in the lives of Jesus and his disciples.

The Bible says Jesus tried to withdraw "to a solitary place" when he heard the news, but crowds of people followed him anyway. And when Jesus saw them, the Bible says "he had compassion on them." He went on to perform one of his most visible miracles—feeding five thousand men, plus women and children, with five loaves of bread and two fish. Sunny skies!

 *Play track 4, "Sunny and Stormy," from the* Essential Messages *CD as a summary of Matthew 14:22-33. Afterward, have groups discuss the following questions:*

*Ask*

- **What do you think Peter was feeling?**

- **When have you had a roller-coaster day like Peter had? What was that like?**

- **When you're trying to navigate these sunny-to-stormy days, how can you keep your focus on Jesus and not let fear and doubt sink you?**

Peter had followed Jesus through a very topsy-turvy day. Each step of the way, Jesus had demonstrated love and power. But there, out on the water with Jesus standing right in front of him, Peter let fear take over. We can learn some valuable lessons from Peter about following Jesus even when life throws stormy weather our way.

## Focus on Jesus

One of Peter's mistakes there on the water was that he shifted his focus off Jesus. He allowed distractions such as the wind to take over and was suddenly aware of his own inability to help himself.

*Invite students to share stories from their own lives of times when losing focus on Jesus had dire consequences.*

God promises never to leave us. *Never.* Yet often, just before God is about to do something totally awesome in and through us, we shift our focus. We get distracted by the wind and waves of this world.

*Ask*

- **What are common circumstances that distract teenagers from focusing on Jesus?**

• **What might help you remember to focus on him?**

Focusing is primarily a matter of trust. Focusing on Jesus means we trust him more than we trust ourselves. Peter trusted Jesus to get him out on the water but then lost trust when he realized he couldn't help himself. This is why "practicing" trust through reading the Bible, praying, and being involved in church is so important. Those activities don't make God love us more, but they help us focus more on God.

If you focus on Jesus, the storms will fade into the background but will *not* go away. Though we can't banish tough circumstances from life, Jesus will reach out his hand to help steady us during those times. If you want to keep from sinking, focus on Jesus.

## Take a Step

Now that we understand the importance of focusing on Jesus, we can learn another lesson from Peter's experience: If you're going to follow Jesus, you have to take a step. Let's get a feel for what this is like.

*Have students form pairs and take turns doing this very simple exercise to experience trust. One partner stands behind the other, and on the count of three, the person in front allows himself or herself to fall backward into the partner's arms. Afterward, have students sit down; then lead a short discussion.*

*Ask*

• **What was it like to fall backward into someone's arms?**

• **Describe a situation in which you had to put your trust in someone else's hands for your own safety. What was that like?**

• **How are your experiences with trust similar to Peter's experience of trusting Jesus?**

*Read aloud Matthew 14:28-29.*

While the other disciples stayed in the boat, Peter took a step. He listened to Jesus and trusted him...and then obeyed. In the same way, Jesus says to us, "Step out of the boat. With me, you can make a difference. Even if you fail, I'll pick you up!"

But you might be saying, "But the boat is safe and comfortable. It's where all my friends hang out. I'm not sure I want to take a chance; it seems too risky." Remember, God promises to help you, to comfort you, to never leave you. That's what you get when you follow Jesus—the Creator of the universe walking with you through every sunny and stormy step of life. With that in mind, trust God enough to take a step!

*Have pairs discuss these questions:*

*Ask*

• **What are some examples of steps you might have to take?**

**BONUS IDEA**

*Use this object lesson to demonstrate the effects of focusing on Jesus.*

*Gather a glass, a pitcher of water, and a mixing bowl. Set the glass inside the mixing bowl.*

Some Christians regard spiritual disciplines as a way to earn brownie points with God. But the truth is that God loves us 100 percent already—just the way we are. So what's the point of spiritual disciplines? To focus on Jesus so that we grow in love for him until we are filled to overflowing with his love.

*Pour water into the glass until the glass overflows—the excess water can pour into the mixing bowl. For full effect, keep letting water overflow from the glass for a number of seconds.*

When we're filled with Jesus' love, it spills out of us and onto other people.

*Sprinkle water from the mixing bowl onto students sitting near you.*

Tell your own "take a step" story. Tell of a time you were frightened but took a step anyway (jumping off a high diving board, bungee jumping). Or tell of a time when you encouraged someone else to take a step. Be sure to choose a story that's full of suspense, interesting circumstances, awkward moments, on so on.

## PARENT CONNECT

Encourage youth to bring up the following conversational questions with their families about Peter's water-walking experience:

• **Why do you think Peter cried out to Jesus when he started to sink?**

• **What can this teach us about placing our trust in Jesus in the midst of storms?**

• **What are the biggest challenges to taking these steps?**

• **How can you conquer these challenges?**

We are all at different places in life, so we won't be taking the same steps. But you will never experience the impossible, fantastic, awesome, unbelievable, risky, totally fulfilling life unless you get out of the boat and take a step.

*Have pairs pray for each other, asking God to grant each other the courage, persistence, and strength to take the steps they just talked about.*

# Wrapping Up

Following Jesus doesn't guarantee a storm-free life. In fact, Peter's life was filled with storms as a disciple. It means focusing on Jesus instead of depending upon your own strength. It means being willing to trust Jesus enough to step toward him, to obey him, to trust and love him.

## DAILY CHALLENGE®

*In their same pairs, have students discuss these questions:*

*Ask*

• **What are the top three distractions that keep you from focusing on Jesus?**

• **What can help you practice focusing on Jesus?**

• **What do you think your life might look like if you were focused on Jesus and trusting him completely even in the midst of storms?**

*Have everyone choose a Daily Challenge they'll follow through on in the days that follow.*

*Ask*

• **What one thing will you commit to doing this week to help you practice focusing on Jesus so you will be better prepared to take steps in his power?**

*Before students leave, remind them to follow through on their Daily Challenge commitment—and to tell someone how it goes.*

# ⑨ Dirty Rotten Scoundrels

## TOPIC
**Forgiveness**

## SCRIPTURE
- Matthew 18:21-35
- Luke 23:34
- Romans 3:9-18, 23-24
- Colossians 3:13

## PURPOSE
To challenge students to accept God's forgiveness and forgive those who hurt them.

## SUPPLIES NEEDED
- *Essential Messages* CD
- CD player
- Bibles
- Paper and pencils
- Art supplies such as markers, crayons, yarn, modeling clay
- A deck of playing cards for every 10 students
- Poster board (one per group of three students)

## SET-UP
- Set up a CD player with the *Essential Messages* CD cued to track 5, "True Confessions."

---

### BONUS IDEA

Divide your meeting area in half. On one side, create a barren ambience with folding chairs. Use this atmosphere to represent the kind of cold isolation we live in when we refuse to let go of a grudge. On the other side of the room, create a cozy atmosphere with comfy seating, candles, plants, coffee tables, framed pictures of friends, music playing, and a plate of cookies. This will represent the warmth and friendship available when we refuse to harbor bitterness toward those who hurt us.

---

## Starting Off
### Villains

*If you choose to do the bonus idea, light the candles and begin the soft music as students arrive. As they enter the room, note where they choose to sit. Most likely, they will assemble in the comfy half of the room. After they've had a chance to visit a bit, eat some cookies, and enjoy the music, begin the message with the following statement.*

You might have noticed that this side of the room is a little more welcoming than that side. Just about all of us enjoy the welcoming warmth of relationships. Yet a lot of people settle for cold isolation in their personal lives when they hold on to a grudge. Let's explore some of the behaviors we find difficult to forgive.

*If you don't choose to do the bonus option, simply welcome students as they arrive.*

*Have students form pairs, and set out art supplies such as paper, pencils, markers, crayons, yarn, modeling clay, and so on. Explain that each pair should use the art supplies to create a villain—an over-the-top, superhero, movie- or comic book–style villain. Each pair also should create a short biography describing the villain's rottenness and explaining how it came to be so mean—what happened to cause such behavior? Emphasize that students are to create totally fictional characters. Give pairs about 10 minutes to work, and then give each a chance to introduce its villain to the rest of the group. Lead a short discussion with the entire group.*

*Ask*

- **What do these villains have in common? What makes them unique?**
- **When has someone acted like a villain toward you?**
- **What was your response?**
- **Why is it so difficult to forgive someone who treated you badly?**

When it comes to forgiveness, it's nice to be on the receiving end. But forgiving someone who has hurt us can be one of the most difficult things to do in life. Today we're going to explore why forgiveness is so important.

# Digging In
## We're All Scoundrels

*Have teenagers return to their pairs. Explain that the challenge this time will be to see how they, too, have acted like villains. Students each should describe an incident in which they acted poorly, describe why they behaved the way they did, and then describe the effect of their behavior on the other people involved.*

*After a few minutes, ask a volunteer to read aloud Romans 3:9-18, 23-24. Then lead a short discussion.*

*Ask*

- **How does God view our sin?**
- **Why do we tend to think that we deserve forgiveness but find it so difficult to forgive others?**

When someone hurts us, we may not stop to consider that we, too, act like creeps sometimes, have bad days, misunderstand, lack sensitivity, and so on. Only when we realize that we are guilty of hurting others can we begin to forgive others for hurting us.

## We've Been Forgiven a Huge Debt

*Have students form circles of about 10 people. Give each group a deck of cards, scraps of paper, and pencils. Tell groups that they'll use the scraps of paper to keep a running tab of debt or credit for each player.*

*Explain that each player begins the game with a balance of zero. Students should pass the deck of cards around the circle, and each participant should remove the top card from the stack. Anyone who draws a black number card receives credit equal to 10 times that number. Anyone who draws a red number card receives debt equal to 10 times that number. For example, an eight of hearts puts a player $80 in the hole, while a five of clubs gives a player $50 of credit. Face cards and jokers are equal to $100. Explain that during the game, you will call out instructions such as "pass your cards to the right" or "reverse the direction of the deck." When a group has divvied up an entire deck of cards, players should tally their balances and determine whether they are in debt or have credit.*

*When everyone understands how to play, have groups begin. While they play, call out instructions every 20 seconds or so — "Pass your cards to the person on your right," "Send the deck in the opposite direction," and so on until all the cards have been taken. Then have groups discuss these questions:*

*Ask*

- **For those of you whose balance indicates you're in debt, what would it be like to owe someone that much money?**

- **For those of you whose balance indicates a credit, what would it be like if someone else owed you that much money?**

- **What other kinds of debts do people face in real life?**

- **What does it feel like when you owe someone financially or otherwise?**

- **What does it feel like when someone owes you?**

*Be sure each student has a Bible, and ask them to read Matthew 18:21-35 silently while picturing themselves as the servant whose enormous debt was forgiven. Then help these verses hit home by summarizing the passage.*

Imagine that you are in debt up to your eyelashes. I'm not talking college loans or even a house mortgage. The servant in this passage owed "ten thousand talents," or millions of dollars. No amount of labor could work off the debt he owed. The only thing of value he had left, his very freedom and the lives of his family, would be sold as he faced a lifetime of slavery.

In a twist of unexpected fortune, the king showed mercy to the servant and "cancelled the debt."

No looking back. No weight around his neck. A chance for a new start. Freedom. This forgiveness was completely liberating in every sense of the word.

The next part of the story seems ludicrous. Immediately upon leaving,

### BONUS IDEA

If you want to, replace an activity with a wild game of mud ball. In a drink pitcher, mix potting soil with water, and then use a wide-tipped funnel to pour the goop into water balloons. Give each participant chances to whack mud-filled balloons with a softball bat. When everyone is mud-caked, use Romans 3:9-18, 23-24 to help students realize that everyone is in need of God's cleansing forgiveness.

the forgiven servant happened upon a poor soul who owed him a hundred denarii, which is the equivalent of a few dollars. The servant who had just been pardoned himself tried to choke a few bucks out of his buddy.

*Have groups discuss these questions:*

*Ask*

- **When have you been more like the king in this story? When have you been more like the servant?**

- **Why did the servant's actions upset the king so much?**

- **Because the king represents God in this parable, what does this say about God's view on forgiveness?**

Look again at your slips of paper. For those of you who are owed, tear up those tabs. For those of you who owe, tear up those tabs. This is exactly what God does for us. No matter what we've done, he erases our tabs when we come to him and seek his forgiveness. What a wonderful, freeing expression of love!

## We Must Forgive Others

*Play track 5, "True Confessions," from the* Essential Messages *CD. Then have students form three groups— the Bradley group, the Audrey group, and the Andrew group—for the following discussion.*

*Ask*

- **How would you have felt if you faced a situation such as the one your character faced?**

- **What might have been your initial response?**

- **How could your character respond to the situation in a way that reflects love and reverence for Christ?**

*After a few minutes for discussion, instruct each group to create a follow-up skit to demonstrate to the rest of the groups how its character could respond to the situation in a loving, Christ-like manner. After a few minutes for skit preparation, have groups perform their skits for one another. Then have students form trios so that each trio includes a member of the Bradley group, the Audrey group, and the Andrew group. Have trios discuss these questions.*

*Ask*

- **Why is it so hard to forgive and trust a friend when he or she hasn't been truthful?**

- **How can Christ help a child recover from the real pain inflicted when a parent abuses, lies to, or belittles him or her?**

- **How did Christ respond to those who hurt him?**

- **What can you learn about forgiveness from his example?**

Christ was betrayed by a couple of his closest friends. He was accused and convicted of something he didn't do. He was beaten by bullies. He was condemned to die by people who had been singing his praises a week earlier. His body was crushed. He was all but abandoned. And what was his response? "Father, forgive them," he said (Luke 23:34).

*Ask a volunteer to read aloud Colossians 3:13.*

I wish there were a way to protect each one of you from pain, but there isn't. When someone betrays you, hurts you, or offends you, your natural inclination may be to respond with anger. But when that moment comes, with all the discipline you can gather, consider what Christ has done for you. Pray that God will help you along the path toward forgiveness.

# Wrapping Up

*In their groups of three, have students create a 10-step program for Bitter-Busters Anonymous entitled "How to Reconcile." These should be practical ideas on how to go about truly reconciling, which is more than saying, "I'm sorry" and "I forgive you." Provide poster board and markers so that groups can present their program as a poster to the other groups. When groups have finished, have them share their work.*

## DAILY CHALLENGE®

*Have students discuss these questions in their groups:*

*Ask*

- **Share a time when you were hurt by someone. How did you work through it?**

- **Has there ever been a time when it seemed too difficult, even impossible, to forgive someone? When you face those circumstances in the future, what can you pray for?**

*Have everyone choose a Daily Challenge they'll follow through on in the days that follow.*

*Ask*

- **What one thing will you commit to doing this week to reconcile with someone you've been avoiding?**

*Have students pray in pairs for God's assistance and understanding when it comes to forgiving others.*

*Before students leave, remind them to follow through on their Daily Challenge commitment—and to tell someone how it goes.*

## TIP FOR THE LEADER

Some of your students may be dealing with unresolved issues that won't be settled in the confines of this lesson. In hurtful situations such as real abuse or neglect, forcing or guilt-tripping a teenager into an insincere "I forgive you" may do more harm than good. Extend an invitation to anyone left scarred to meet in a more private, less threatening environment. Be prepared with the resources at your disposal—check your church's library for books on abuse and forgiveness and even have the name of a Christian counselor on hand. Have both male and female church members in mind who could befriend these students and help them work through their pain slowly and delicately so forgiveness is a natural outpouring of the healing that is taking place. Match students with adults of the same gender who would be excellent spiritual mentors. Perhaps even those who have worked through a similar wound.

# Things Friends Do

4/15/12

## TOPIC
**Friendship**

## SCRIPTURE
- Romans 12:10; 15:1-2, 7
- Ephesians 4:2-3, 31-32
- 1 Thessalonians 5:11
- Hebrews 10:24-25
- 1 Peter 3:8-9

## PURPOSE
To help students develop strong, authentic friendships.

## SUPPLIES NEEDED
- *Essential Messages* CD
- CD player
- Bibles
- Newsprint, masking tape, markers
- Index cards
- Paper and pens
- Crayons
- Blank mailing labels or stickers

## SET-UP
- Set up the CD player with the *Essential Messages* CD cued to audio track 6, "Friendly Prayer."

---

### TIP FOR THE LEADER

If you have more than 20 students, give students one card each, and ask half to write one thing friends do and the others to write one thing friends don't do. Then let the two groups rank each category. This will save time.

## Starting Off
### A Friend Indeed

I'm sure we'd all agree that friendship involves give-and-take; sometimes you have something to offer, and other times you need something. So we're going to begin this message on friendship by giving and receiving some information from our friends about how good friends act and don't act—or, in other words, things friends do and things friends don't do.

*Ask students to form four groups, and give each person two index cards and a pen. Ask students to quietly write one thing friends do on one card (i.e., friends are nice to each other) and one thing friends don't do on the other (i.e., friends don't gossip about each other).*

*Next, ask group members to work together to rank their answers by how many people answered the same way. For example, three people said friends are nice, two people said friends are flexible, and one person*

## TIP FOR THE LEADER

Sharing illustrations from your own friendships will definitely enhance this message!

said friends share. Groups should have two piles of index cards: one for things friends do and one for things friends don't do.

Tape a sheet of newsprint to a wall. Lead groups in compiling two ranked lists of things friends do and things friends don't do. Work toward a top-five list for each category, understanding that your lists might be longer if you have time and enough students. Starting with the "Things Friends Do" category, ask the group who has the most votes for one action to name that action first. Then ask other groups if they had that same action or something similar. On the newsprint, record the actions and the number of people who listed each action.

Ask

- **Do you agree with the rank these friendship characteristics received? Explain.**

- **What can we learn from a quick scan of each list?**

You did a great job on these lists! You obviously know a lot about how to be good friends. Today's message will highlight just a few "Things Friends Do."

# Digging In

Assign each of the four groups one of the message points and its accompanying Scripture passages. Tell groups they have five minutes to read and discuss their passages then come up with two quick scenarios they will act out when you get to that point in the message: what it looks like when friends don't act that way and what it looks like when they do.

## Friends Accept Each Other

Ask for two volunteers from the first group to read Romans 15:7 and Ephesians 4:2-3 before the group enacts its two scenarios. Lead students in applauding the group's performance.

Let's be honest: The people we call "friends" are people we like. You know how some people just click? Our friends tend to be the people we click with. Of course you can develop friendships with people who are very different from you, people with whom you didn't initially click, you might say. Still, by the time you call these people friends, you like them.

Honest point No. 2: Everyone does something that annoys someone else. Some twirl their hair, some say "y'know," some crack their knuckles...No matter how much you like your friends and they like you, you will annoy each other sometimes.

But friends also accept each other. Friends are patient, putting up with our habits and faults. Friends are gentle, even when they don't want to be. Friends who are also Christians accept each other in a spirit of unity and peace because Jesus accepted all of us even when we weren't clicking with God. Friendship and unity are more important than the annoying things we all do. Sometimes it's easy. Other times it's hard work. Either way, friends accept each other.

## Friends Encourage Each Other

*Ask for two volunteers from the second group to read 1 Thessalonians 5:11 and Hebrews 10:24-25 before the group enacts its two scenarios. Lead students in applauding the group's performance.*

Think back through your day and count how many times you heard someone say something negative. Now count how many times you heard someone say something kind. Could anyone count more kind words than negative?

Life can be hard. People are under a lot of pressure to feel good about themselves, to be successful, often just to keep their heads above water. And too often the things people say reflect their own stress. So our ears fill up with negatives. Unfortunately, unless those comments are balanced by an awful lot of positive comments, we may begin to believe all the negative things we hear about ourselves, our lives, and our world.

That's why it is so, so, so important for friends to encourage each other. It may be way too easy to make flippant and cutting remarks, but as friends, we need to resist that temptation in order to provide the positive balance we all so desperately need. Rather than tear each other down, or letting life's hard circumstances tear our friends down, we have the privilege to build each other up and help each other commit purposeful acts of love and kindness.

*Give each group a sheet of newsprint and markers. Ask groups to create two columns on their sheets of newsprint. Explain that in one column, they are to list acts of love and good deeds teenagers can do. In the other column, they can list ways they can encourage their friends ("spur one another on") to do those things. For example, a good deed might be serving at a soup kitchen once a month, and teenagers could call a friend the day before the soup kitchen to remind the friend to come and serve.*

*Ask*

- **What's the difference between encouraging a friend to do good deeds and encouraging a friend by making them feel good? How are they similar?**

Whether we are encouraging our friends by telling them we think they're great or encouraging them to do good things, things that will honor God, we are building them up. Besides, encouraging our friends to do good deeds will ultimately help them to feel good about themselves as well. It's a win-win situation.

> ## BONUS IDEA
>
> If there are any senior adults in your church who have been friends since they were teenagers, or who have friends they met as teenagers, invite them to attend this meeting and share with the students what they did and didn't do to maintain the friendships. Be sure to have them highlight the role a relationship with Jesus Christ played in their friendships.

## Friends Forgive Each Other

*Ask for two volunteers from the third group to read Romans 15:1-2 and Ephesians 4:31-32 before the group enacts its two scenarios. Lead students in applauding the group's performance.*

Forgiveness may be one of the hardest things friends do for one another, but it may also be one of the most important. We've already talked about how we will all annoy each other sometimes, but this goes much deeper. We will all mess up in our friendships at some point. Whether we betray a confidence or fail to keep a promise, somehow we will let our friends down and they will let us down.

That's guaranteed. And it helps to decide in advance whether you will be the kind of friend who is willing to work at forgiveness. You see, lack of forgiveness hurts not only the person who needs forgiving but also the friendship—and you! By choosing not to forgive, you decide to hold yourself in bondage to the anger that you could release with God's help.

Forgiveness does not mean that the offense never happened, and forgiveness doesn't make the offense go away. Instead, forgiveness means choosing not to hold on to the negative emotions and being willing to live with the consequences without demanding that your friend also experience penalty.

For example, if you borrow my cell phone and run up a monster-size bill, I may ask you to pay the bill. I may not let you borrow my cell phone again. But if I forgive you, I will not continue to be angry. I will not talk badly about you to others or make sarcastic comments about your lack of responsibility. Make sense? There are consequences to your action, but I limit my *reaction*. I don't make the situation worse in my anger. By forgiving you, I am able to deal with the situation rationally and am able to mend the friendship with kindness.

*Give students paper and crayons, and ask them to silently write words that reflect any bitterness, rage, and anger they hold toward others. Ask them to bring those emotions to God in confession. Then give teenagers blank mailing labels or stickers which they can place over each word. On the stickers they can write words of kindness, compassion, and love, asking that God would help them to replace the former emotions/actions with these new emotions/actions.*

## Friends Stick Together

*Ask for two volunteers from the final group to read Romans 12:10 and 1 Peter 3:8-9 before the group enacts its two scenarios. Lead students in applauding the group's performance.*

How many of you have a brother or sister? Well, obviously not all sibling relationships are great models of strong, healthy friendships, but they have something in common: No matter what you do or where you go, there is nothing you can do to change the reality that you and your sibling are related by blood. Even if you could get a legal document stating that you are not siblings, you can't change the biology. Friends should initiate that kind of stick-togetherness.

As we stick together—as we love and honor each other—we will all be loved, and we will all be honored.

Being devoted to each other in love, sticking together, involves all the other points we've talked about—accepting each other, encouraging each other, and forgiving each other. It means living out your friendship even when you don't feel it. Maybe especially then. Because friendship is easy when everything's happy-go-lucky and the world is rosy, but friendship is tested when things get tough. Those times you have to stick together no matter what.

# Wrapping Up

*Lead a short discussion.*

*Ask*

- **Which of these four friendship habits can you apply to your friendship with Jesus? Explain how.**

- **How do you think becoming a better friend to others could strengthen your friendship with Jesus?**

*Have teenagers find spots by themselves around the meeting area, and explain that they're going to participate in a prayerful mediation led by the CD.*

 *Play track 6, "Friendly Prayer," from the* Essential Messages *CD as teenagers follow along silently. Afterward, have students form pairs.*

# DAILY CHALLENGE®

*Ask students to share with a partner how they would rate themselves on a scale of 1-5 (1 is poor, 5 is great) on each of the four friendship habits. Then ask partners to work together to develop a goal to strengthen the habit on which they scored the lowest. For example, they could write one encouraging e-mail to a friend every day or forgive someone they've held a grudge against.*

*Ask*

• **What one thing will you commit to doing to become a better friend this week?**

Most of us think of friendships as essential, adding so much joy to life. We often forget that being a good friend requires a lot of hard, consistent work. But with Jesus as our model and friend, and with commitment on our part, we can become better friends and add to the joy friendships bring to our lives.

*Before students leave, remind them to follow through on their Daily Challenge commitment—and to tell someone how it goes.*

# Don't Label Me!

*1/29/12*

## TOPIC
**Identity**

## SCRIPTURE
- 1 Samuel 16:1, 5-13; 17:1-58; 18:2, 5-7
- 2 Samuel 11–12
- Psalm 139:13-16
- Romans 3:23-24; 6:23

## PURPOSE
To equip students to peel off the labels others place on them, and discover the significance of their true identity (people loved and highly valued by God).

## SUPPLIES NEEDED
- *Essential Messages* CD
- Bibles
- Adhesive labels
- Newsprint, masking tape, and markers
- Pencils and erasers
- TV, VCR/DVD player, and *Les Misérables* video/DVD (Columbia/TriStar Studios, 1998)

## SET-UP
- Print enough copies of the "Person" handout from *Essential Messages* CD for each student to have one.

- Write different descriptions of people on the adhesive labels, such as "senior citizen," "druggie," "the president," "doctor," "homeless person," "kindergartener," "math teacher," and "millionaire." You'll need to create enough labels so that every teenager will have one.

- Set up the TV and VCR/DVD player, and cue *Les Misérables* to approximately 0:06:50 (if you're using a VCR, set the counter to 0:00:00 when the studio logo appears). Preview the clip at least once before students arrive.

- Tape a sheet of newsprint to a wall.

## Starting Off
### Label Me

Everybody wears identity labels. And society uses these labels to determine how each person should be treated. We're going to play a game called "Label Me."

*Affix an adhesive label to each student's back.*

You've got five minutes to mingle and talk with each other. When you talk to someone, check his or her label, and then treat that person

according to what you read. For example, if someone's label is "the president," you'd treat that person with great respect and honor. You can't give others clues or directly tell them what is on their labels. You can only give hints by the way you treat them. For example, if someone is labeled "kindergartener," you might try to teach that person the alphabet. At the end of five minutes of mingling, you each get a chance to guess what your label is.

*Answer any questions teenagers might have; then prompt them to start mingling. When time's up, have teenagers pair up and guess what their identities are. They can then remove their labels to discover the correct answers.*

*Have everyone sit down; then lead the group in a discussion.*

*Ask*

- **How did people treat you during this activity?**

- **If this were your true identity, how would you feel about yourself?**

- **Do people label you in real life? If so, how?**

We all wear labels. Some are positive labels that we enjoy, like "popular," "talented," or "smart." Others are negative, hurtful labels that we wish we could peel off, like "failure," "weird," or "average."

Our identities aren't found in labels. Though society values labels, they're meaningless to God. Labels don't tell the truth about us. Labels aren't the sources of our identities. Labels are meant to be peeled right off.

# Digging In

We're going to take some time to look at the life of a guy who wore lots of different labels during his life: David (he was a king in the Old Testament).

*Write the words "David's Labels" at the top of the newsprint sheet you taped to a wall.*

## God Looks at the Heart

Despite all the different labels his family and society put on him, David knew the truth: God looks at the heart. He found his identity in God and God alone.

*Invite volunteers to read aloud 1 Samuel 16:1, 5-13.*

The first label David wore was the "Insignificant Little Brother."

*Write "Insignificant Little Brother" on the newsprint.*

He was young and small. He was viewed as so insignificant that his dad didn't even think of him when he first gathered the brothers to be examined by the prophet Samuel.

Yet check out what happened! Despite the label, despite how unimportant he seemed to his family and society, God chose David to be king! 1 Samuel 16:7 says, "Man looks at the outward appearance, but the Lord looks at the heart." That "Insignificant Little Brother" label meant nothing to God. He looked at the heart and saw the real David.

Let's look at another label people stuck on David.

*Summarize all of 1 Samuel 17:1-37, and then have a volunteer read aloud 1 Samuel 17:28-29, 33.*

The second label David wore was the "Untrained, Unaccomplished Fighter."

*Write "Untrained, Unaccomplished Fighter" on the newsprint.*

David was determined to stand up for God against Goliath, but all his brothers and Saul saw was David's young age and his lack of military experience. Goliath was the best fighter the Philistines had—how could Israel send out a young kid without any accomplishments? He didn't even have his own armor!

But you probably know the rest of the story.

*Summarize 1 Samuel 17:38-58.*

Surprise, surprise. This twerpy, untrained kid took out the attacking army's greatest fighter. See, Saul and the others weren't looking at the right things. They just saw the label, but God saw the truth about David. God saw David's passionate and courageous heart. David's social status and lack of accomplishments didn't mean anything to God. That silly label didn't stick.

Let's check out one more label society stuck on David.

*Invite a volunteer to read aloud 1 Samuel 18:2, 5-7.*

Interesting, huh? Now that insignificant, untrained kid has become Mr. Popularity to the Israelites. One little giant-slaying, and suddenly they view David completely differently.

The third label David wore was the "Accomplished, Popular Hero."

*Write "Accomplished, Popular Hero" on the newsprint.*

This is a pretty cool label to wear. I'm sure David enjoyed being viewed this way! But here's the thing: David's popularity and accomplishments weren't a big deal to God. God still looked at one thing: David's heart.

*Review the three labels you've written on the newsprint.*

How about you? What labels do you wear? Can you relate to any of these? I'd like you to think for a moment about these questions: How do you view yourself? How does your family view you? How do others view you? What positive or negative labels have been stuck on you?

*Distribute a "Person" handout and a pencil to each student. Invite*

## TIP FOR THE LEADER

It is important that students use pencils during this activity, not pens. Why? Because later on they'll need to erase what they've written.

teenagers to read the instructions and then take some time to write labels on their person outlines.

*After a few minutes, direct teenagers to form pairs and share what they wrote on their handouts with their partners, explaining the various labels.*

God looks at the heart, but what about when your heart is blackened by sin? Let's look at another label David wore.

*Summarize the events of 2 Samuel 11–12. Then write these words on the newsprint: "Adulterer, Murderer, Sinner."*

Now David's actions labeled him in a different way. He was an adulterer. He was a murderer. He was a sinner, just like us.

*Instruct teenagers to use their pencils to draw a blackened heart on their "Person" handout.*

## We Are Not Defined by Our Sin

Just like David, our hearts are blackened by sin. But there's good news: Our identities do not need to be found in sin and guilt.

*To make a point about how sin does not need to define us, show a clip from* Les Misérables. *If you're using a VCR, set the counter to 0:00:00 when the studio logo appears. Begin the clip at approximately 0:06:50 when Jean Valjean starts putting the silverware into his sack. End the clip at approximately 0:09:50 when the scene fades to black.*

In this scene we see a man, Jean Valjean, who is labeled by his sin. He's an ex-con who has attacked a kind priest and stolen his silver. To society he is no more than a worthless thief.

You may feel like Jean Valjean. You may have done something that's made you feel so guilty, so low, that you've labeled yourself as worthless. You may be struggling with a sin, and you've labeled yourself as a failure. You don't see hope for yourself. You can't see who you really are.

But the priest in this scene refuses to let Jean Valjean find his identity in his guilt. The priest forgives Jean Valjean and shows him who he really is—a person who is valuable to God.

*Invite volunteers to read aloud Romans 3:23-24; 6:23.*

Like Jean Valjean, we can be forgiven by God. God loves us!

## God Made Us and Loves Us—
## That's Our True Identity

God doesn't look at our outsides, our families' expectations of us, our accomplishments, our popularity, or our sin. Instead he sees us as special and valuable. Why? Because God made us! We are extremely valuable to him. Let's read something our friend David wrote later in his life.

*Invite a volunteer to read aloud Psalm 139:13-16.*

 The maker of the galaxies, the stars, the mountains, and the oceans *made you.* God loves you, no matter what. And this fact is where you can find your true identity: You are made and loved by God. All the labels people place on you are insignificant compared to this one truth.

# Wrapping Up

*Distribute erasers and invite teenagers to illustrate the meaninglessness of labels by erasing all the labels they've written on their "Person" handout. Also have them erase the blackened heart, symbolizing God's forgiveness of their sin. Then distribute markers.*

Let's take some time to celebrate our true identities as individuals made and loved by God. Use your marker to create a personal identity statement and write it on your "Person" outline. Start out by writing "I am..." and then add anything else you want to say. You could paraphrase a verse from Psalm 139, write down one of the points from this message, or just make something up using your own words.

*When they're done with their personal identity statements, have teenagers re-form their pairs from earlier in the message. Prompt them to share their handouts with their partners and explain why they wrote what they did.*

 When people stick labels on you, positive or negative, you need to peel them right off. That's not your true identity! When you struggle with sin, you can peel that label off, too, by seeking God's forgiveness. That's not your true identity! No matter what happens to you in your life, no matter what others may say or think about you, always hold on to this truth: You are made and loved by God. *That's* the true identity you can hold on to in your heart.

---

**BONUS IDEA**

This topic is so crucial during the teenage years! Consider using this content to create an overnight lock-in or a two-night weekend retreat. Expand the teaching sessions and add activities such as having teenagers create collages with magazine pictures to represent their identities. Include times for personal journaling, and show the full *Les Misérables* video. Use the movie as a launching pad to discuss sin, grace, and true identity.

# DAILY CHALLENGE®

*Have teenagers form groups of two or three to discuss these questions:*

> *Ask*

- **Why is it important to find your true identity in God? How could that impact your daily life?**

- **How has this message impacted your view of yourself?**

*Have everyone choose a Daily Challenge they'll follow through on in the days that follow.*

> *Ask*

- **What one thing will you commit to doing to remove false identity labels and stand tall in your true identity?**

*Have teenagers pray for each other within their groups. Then close in prayer, asking God to help students peel off the false identity labels in their lives and instead find confidence and joy in their identities as creatures made and loved by God.*

*Before students leave, remind them to follow through on their Daily Challenge commitment—and to tell someone how it goes.*

## PARENT CONNECT

Challenge teenagers to hunt down and find a picture of their parent(s) as a teenager. Once they've found one, they should show it to their parents and laugh a bit together. The picture is sure to be pretty hilarious! Prompt teenagers to use the picture as a discussion starter as they find out more about what each parent's life was like as an adolescent. Have teenagers ask about the "labels" their parents wore as a teenager and how they compare or contrast with what the parent is really like.

This activity will help parents and teenagers connect with each other as they discuss how the teenage years are a critical stage of identity development. The parents went through it, too! This will give parents the opportunity to encourage their teenagers and remind them that God loves them through the whole process of discovering who they really are.

# ⑫ Changing Views

4/29/12

## TOPIC

**Prayer**

## SCRIPTURE

■ Matthew 6:9-13

## PURPOSE

To help students understand why and how to pray so they can commit to communicate intimately with God.

## SUPPLIES NEEDED

■ *Essential Messages* CD
■ Bibles
■ Pens and pencils
■ Creative supplies such as clay, paper, pastels, markers, tape, scissors, chenille wire, and craft foam
■ Two 4x6-inch pieces of aluminum foil per student

## SET-UP

■ Print enough copies of the "Prayer Guide" from the *Essential Messages* CD for everyone to have one.

■ Cut aluminum foil into 4x6-inch pieces.

## Starting Off
### It's All About Perspective

*Ask teenagers to tilt their heads to one side and look around, paying attention to the different perspective. Ask them to bend in half and look at things through their legs or crouch down, again noticing the different perspective. After three or four minutes, lead a discussion.*

*Ask*

• **What did you notice about being in a different position?**

• **How does looking at things differently change the way you live?**

Just as a different body posture can give us a different view of the world, prayer is a different "spiritual" posture that changes our view and ultimately changes us.

# Digging In

*Ask teenagers to form small groups as you distribute pens, Bibles, and the "Prayer Guide" handouts.*

Today we're going to talk about prayer, and we'll involve prayer experiences every step of the way. Of course we can always come to God with anything, any rantings or ravings that need airing, any chaos that needs order. But Jesus taught his disciples to pray, and both the specific content and the order of that prayer can help us know what to pray and how to pray more effectively.

*Give teenagers a minute to take deep breaths and quiet themselves, and then read Matthew 6:9-13 together.*

## Prayer Changes Our View of God

*Read aloud Matthew 6:9.*

Jesus begins his prayer by addressing "Our Father." Right from the start, we have some information about God. He is not just *my* Father, but *ours*. When I remember that this God I'm praying to loves you as much as me—and the people across the world as much as us—well, then I remember that this is one big, loving God!

And God is our "Father," but this dad has all the best attributes of parenthood, better than any human mother and father. We get a glimpse of why that is when we pray, "in heaven." Our Father in heaven is with us like a parent, but he's also above it all and can see the big picture. I might get stuck in my perspective, but God doesn't.

Whew! One little phrase, and already our heads are spinning with our view of God! So what's next?

"Hallowed be your name." God is holy. I mess up again and again, but God never does. God is always good, always perfect, and that never changes. So when we pray, we praise God for who he is right off the bat. We pay attention to God and the relationship we have with God. Prayer changes our view of God as we focus on who God is and what God has done.

*Ask small groups to brainstorm and write in their prayer guides specific things to praise and thank God for—for example, God's goodness and creation or God's love and salvation. When teenagers have finished, ask groups to use the creative supplies you've provided to create something that represents who God is and what God has done. Everyone needs to be involved in the creative process. After a few minutes, ask groups to share what they created and why.*

## Prayer Changes Our View of What's Important

*Read aloud Matthew 6:10-11.*

Jesus worships and praises God first then asks for what God wants. The emphasis is on God's kingdom and will, not ours. Too often we rush into prayer with a long list of wants. Maybe that's all our prayers are sometimes. But Jesus' prayer teaches us to hold off on our wants until we've prayed about what God wants. Going this route will probably change our wants! Notice that Jesus asks for "daily bread"—only the food we need to survive this day rather than a portable music system or even a secure future. By teaching us to depend on God for the things we need for *today*, Jesus teaches us to rely on God for everything. And of course, relying on God for everything from today's needs to God's plan for all our tomorrows ultimately is so much more important than whether I have an awesome MP3 player.

*Instruct teenagers to work with a partner to talk about and list their wants and God's wants in the next section of the Prayer Guide. Afterward, have them discuss the following questions:*

*Ask*

- **Which of my wants could also be God's wants? Which don't make the cut? Why?**

- **What can I do to align my wants with God's wants?**

*After a few minutes, ask volunteers to briefly share what they discussed. Then pray together for what God wants.*

## Prayer Changes Our View of Ourselves

*Read aloud Matthew 6:12-13.*

It's really easy to go through the day thinking, *I'm doing just fine. No problems here, thank you very much.* But these verses confront me with a different, less attractive view of myself. I have debts (sins); I need forgiveness; I need to forgive others; I'm also tempted and need God's deliverance from evil. I can't think I'm so good when clearly I desperately need God in order to do anything good.

This is hard stuff, ugly stuff even, and definitely stuff I'd rather not look at too closely or for too long. But as I keep looking, I realize that I'm carrying a lot of baggage that Jesus would like to take from me. As I name the bags and give them to Jesus, I can't believe how much lighter my whole body feels and how much joy fills the parts of me that once felt so burdened. God's forgiveness offers us tremendous freedom.

*Give each person a piece of aluminum foil, and tell them the foil represents a mirror. Ask teenagers to imagine looking in the mirror and seeing their reflection. Next ask them to use a pencil to write on the foil sins they need to confess, initials of people they have yet to forgive,*

**TIP FOR THE LEADER**

The traditional ending of the Lord's Prayer—"For thine is the kingdom, and the power, and the glory, forever. Amen"—is found in some ancient biblical manuscripts but not the most reliable manuscripts from which the Bible was translated. Therefore it is not included in Scripture, even though it has been part of Christian tradition and practice for centuries. If it is appropriate for your group to include this phrase, please do so.

**TIP FOR THE LEADER**

Throughout the interactive and active portions of this message, remind teenagers that they are praying. Break the box of "you have to be still and quiet (i.e., boring) to pray" thinking, and allow for a fresh vision of prayer as a conversation and relationship with a very active God.

Since many worship songs are really prayers that we sing, consider incorporating musical worship into each point of this message. For the first point, use songs that offer thanksgiving and praise to God. For the second point, use songs that ask God for things he wants—justice, mercy, righteousness, and so on. For the third point, use songs that focus on confession.

### TIP FOR THE LEADER

If you have the money, buy compact mirrors and give one to each student in return for their messed-up pieces of foil paper.

### PARENT CONNECT

Many people find praying out loud intimidating. Help families feel more comfortable praying together with this simple prayer starter.

Family members name items to pray about. Using a marker, they write one prayer item on the end of a clean Popsicle stick. Each family member should contribute three or more ideas. Ideas can include friends or family, teachers, health, or world events. Popsicle sticks should be stored in a clean container. Once a week at dinnertime (or more often), each person draws two sticks and prays out loud for those two prayer concerns.

*or temptations they need God's help to resist. When they've finished, ask them to notice how ineffective the mirror would be with all those scratches and tears. The image is distorted.*

*Ask teenagers to silently consider their foils and give God each thing they've written. After a minute or so of quiet, invite them to come forward and trade their marked-up foil for a clean piece to tape into their prayer guides.*

You traded your messed-up "mirror" and your messed-up reflection for a clean mirror and a cleaner reflection. When we confess our sins to God, God restores us, not just in vision but in reality. Prayer changes our view of ourselves, both by allowing us to see the places where we need God to work, but then also by allowing us to see the work God has done and will do in our lives. Prayer changes us!

# Wrapping Up

All right, now it's time to make some decisions. In a minute I'm going to let you discuss in small groups how you can pray in each of these three areas every day. For instance, you could look at nature for examples of God's creativity or think about your day for examples of God's presence. You could pray one psalm every day or search the Bible for what it says about some of the things you want. Or you might commit to pray the Lord's Prayer every day, considering the three points we've talked about as you say the words. As you chat with your group, try to come up with doable ideas and tie them specifically to the three points we've talked about.

## DAILY CHALLENGE®

*Give small groups a few minutes to talk; then ask individuals to take three minutes, one minute per area, and choose one new thing in each area to try this week. Instruct teenagers to write this in the Daily Challenge section of their prayer guides.*

*Ask*

• **What one thing will you commit to doing this week to allow prayer to change you?**

*Close by praying the Lord's Prayer aloud together.*

*Before teenagers leave, remind them to follow through on their Daily Challenge commitment—and to tell someone how it goes.*

# Sex: God's Great Idea

**TOPIC**

**Sexuality**

**SCRIPTURE**

- Genesis 2:24
- Song of Songs 1:2, 15-16; 8:6-7a
- Matthew 5:27-28; 19:4-6
- 1 Corinthians 6:9-11, 18-20; 10:13
- Philippians 4:6-8
- 1 Thessalonians 4:3-7
- 1 John 1:9

**PURPOSE**

To help students develop a healthy biblical view of sexuality and successfully commit to sexual abstinence before marriage.

## SUPPLIES NEEDED

- *Essential Messages* CD
- CD player
- Bibles
- Hot, fresh pizza, and other yummy snacks; drinks, paper plates, paper towels, and cups
- Paper and pens
- Four pillar candles, matches, small candles (one per student), and candle drip guards (one per student)

## SET-UP

- Set up your CD player with the *Essential Messages* CD cued to track 7, "Thoughts About Sex."
- Put a table in the front of the room and set out pizza, other snacks, and drinks.
- Affix drip guards to each small candle that you'll give to students during the "Wrapping Up" prayer activity.

---

**TIP FOR THE LEADER**

This is a sensitive and challenging topic, so it is vital that the parents of your students are on board with you. Arrange a parent meeting one week before you present this message. Share all of the material with them and answer any questions they may have. Let parents know you value their support and that your goal is to help them raise their children as strong Christian men and women.

## Starting Off

*As teenagers are arriving, begin setting up your table of hot pizza, other delicious snacks, and cups of refreshing drinks. Instruct students to take a seat.*

As you can see, I've got some great food for us to enjoy tonight. But we're not going to eat it until the end of the meeting, OK?

First what I'd like you to do is find a partner and take five minutes to talk about this question:

*Ask*

• **What was the best part of your day today? Why?**

*When five minutes are up, gather everyone back together.*

Mmm...doesn't that food smell delicious? If you're like me, you

In addition to the parent meeting you had before this study to review the message content and answer parents' questions, get parents involved through prayer. Ask parents to set aside time during this youth meeting to pray for all the students. Prompt them to pray not only for their own teenagers, but also for those students whose parents might not be Christians. Suggest that parents pray that teenagers will be mature in their behavior, receptive to the message, and that their lives will be impacted. This is a very serious and sensitive issue for teenagers—ample prayer is needed!

Also, advise parents to give their teenagers lots of "space" when they come home from the meeting. They probably won't want to jump into a conversation with mom or dad about sex right away! In fact, some might not want to discuss it at all! Others may have questions or concerns, so parents should be ready to talk if their child initiates the conversation.

were probably distracted by the food during the last five minutes. After all, God gave you an appetite, the senses of taste and smell, and the biological urge of hunger. It probably seems crazy for me to make you wait until the end of the meeting to eat the food! Well, I've changed my mind—you can have some now.

*Have teenagers get some food and sit back down to eat. When everyone is settled, continue your message.*

## We Are Sexual Beings

Just as God made us with physical senses of hunger and appetite, he made all of us as sexual beings. Sexual development and sexual desire are not only biologically normal, they are also closely tied to our emotions and sense of self—and are created by God.

Yet sometimes as teenagers you may feel a bit like you might have felt about the pizza a few minutes ago. The Bible and the church tell you that you have to wait for sex, and yet the whole time you're experiencing those natural sexual desires. Sometimes it feels just plain stupid to wait, when your body, mind, or emotions tell you to go for it. And it doesn't help when friends, TV, music—basically the whole world—is telling you the same thing!

Today we're going to talk about this complex and challenging subject: sexuality.

# Digging In
## Sex Was God's Great Idea

It may seem like Hollywood or MTV are the experts on sexuality, but the truth is that *God* created sex—and he created it to be a good thing! God made us as sexual beings, and he created sex to be enjoyed in the context of marriage.

*Hold up your Bible.*

The Bible has quite a lot to say about sex. The first foundational reference to sex in the Bible is when God created Adam and Eve.

*Read aloud Genesis 2:24.*

We can see here that sex is meant to be a bonding experience between a husband and a wife—a mysterious union that makes the two become one. Jesus also talked about this spiritual union between a husband and a wife in Matthew 19.

*Read aloud Matthew 19:4-6.*

But there's more to it than that—the Bible also speaks of the passion, romantic love, and enjoyment that are part of sexual intimacy. Let me read you just a few verses from Song of Songs, a poetic conversation between a husband and wife.

*Read aloud Song of Songs 1:2, 15-16; and 8:6-7a.*

These are some of the "safer" verses—some parts of Song of Songs are so racy that at one time, Jewish teenagers were forbidden from reading it!

Many people have an improper understanding of Christianity and sexuality. Some think that the church or God views sex as dirty and sinful, while others think that Christianity teaches that sex isn't meant to be enjoyed. Both of these perspectives are dead wrong! We can see from Scripture that sex was God's great idea and that he created it to be good. God also created it to be expressed in one context: within a marriage between a man and a woman.

**TIP FOR THE LEADER**

Teenagers will probably complain that you're making them wait to eat—that's OK. In fact, that's good! You'll use their hunger as an illustration in a few minutes. For now just keep telling them that they need to wait until the end of the meeting. Don't provide any other explanation or rationale.

## But It's Not Always That Simple...

It's easy to talk about the "churchy" view of sex and "God's rules" about waiting until you're married, but the reality is that sexuality is a complex issue with lots of gray areas, lots of questions, and lots of confusion. You may have questions about sexuality that you'll never ask anybody—but it's likely that your questions are normal and common to other people's experiences. Let's listen to some private teenage questions and concerns about sexuality.

*Play "Thoughts About Sex" (track 7) from the Essential Messages CD. Invite teenagers to close their eyes while they listen to it if they'd like to. After the track is finished, continue with your message.*

These questions and concerns are common, and you've likely thought about some of them yourself. The Bible doesn't directly address many of these complex issues and challenging experiences, but it does give us some basic principles that can guide our thinking in these areas. Let's read some passages that can apply to the sexuality questions we just heard.

*Invite several teenage volunteers to read the following Scripture passages aloud: Matthew 5:27-28; 1 Corinthians 6:18-20, 10:13; Philippians 4:6-8; 1 Thessalonians 4:3-7; and 1 John 1:9.*

Based on what you've just heard from Scripture, what kind of advice would you give to the teenagers with questions and concerns that we heard on the CD? How would you apply the truths from the Bible to these challenging situations? Imagine you are a Christian counselor and one of these teenagers is talking to you about his or her situation—what would you say? I'm going to play the audio track one more time, and as you listen, I'd like you to select one of the situations to focus on. After we listen, you'll have some time to write a letter of advice to that student.

**TIP FOR THE LEADER**

This audio track addresses serious sexual issues, including masturbation, pornography, and same-sex attraction. If you have some students in your group who like to goof off, remind everyone to treat these issues as mature adults and to listen to the CD with a respectful attitude.

Play a short clip from the movie *Mean Girls* (Paramount, 2004) to launch this part of the message. If you're using a VCR, set the counter to 0:00:00 when the studio logo appears at the start of the film. Start the clip at approximately 0:06:45 when Cady thinks to herself, *I guess I'll never know what I missed on that first day of health class.* End the clip at approximately 0:07:05 when the scene returns to Cady sitting on the grass with her friends. This clip parodies a high school health class in which the teacher's basic message is: Don't have sex because it could kill you.

This clip is pretty close to what teenagers actually experience in their school health class! By showing this clip, you'll get teenagers to loosen up and laugh a bit about this difficult topic. You can use this humorous and exaggerated clip to make the point that there are lots of competing messages about sex, but only one message is true: God created sexuality.

*Play "Thoughts About Sex" (track 7) again. As you do, distribute paper and pens. When the track is over, tell students to take up to 10 minutes to write a letter of advice to one of the teenagers. They should identify the specific issue the teenager is dealing with and then write as if they were a Christian counselor who is trying to help the student. Assure students that their letters will be completely private— no one else will see what they write.*

*After they've finished, encourage them to fold up their papers and put them with their other belongings.*

## It's Tough but Not Impossible!

The reality is that it is pretty tough to live out a Christ-honoring understanding of sexuality in today's world! We not only have our own natural sexual urges and feelings to deal with, but friends and the media constantly bombard us with more and more distorted messages about sex!

Yes, it's tough to live out God's plan—but it is not impossible. The first thing you can do to live out God's plan is to develop a healthy self-image, grounded in a biblical understanding of sexuality. We need to see ourselves for who we really are: sexual beings. When you have sexual thoughts and feelings, you need to know that it's OK—God made you that way! You don't need to be ashamed of how God made you. At the same time, your view of your sexuality needs to have a firm foundation in Scripture, knowing that though God made you with sexual feelings, he set limits upon how that sexuality is to be expressed. Your view of sex should match scriptural teaching: Sex is a good thing—created for the context of marriage.

The second way you can live out God's plan for your sexuality is to commit to sexual abstinence before marriage. When you're dating, be realistic about physical expressions of affection. Since you know God created you with sexual urges, don't underestimate the realistic danger of one thing leading to another. Instead, set healthy boundaries for what you will and will not do physically. And this doesn't just apply to dating relationships—some of those "gray" areas of sexuality also require boundaries, especially in regard to your thought life. Guard your sexuality—both your thoughts and actions—and commit to choose God's plan by waiting for sex until you're married.

A third really important application step is to understand that God forgives sexual sin. Did you hear me? *God forgives sexual sin.*

*Read aloud 1 Corinthians 6:9-11.*

It doesn't matter what sexual sin you may have committed. It doesn't need to define you. Paul tells the Corinthian Christians who had once led lives of sexual sin, "that is what some of you *were*." They have been forgiven! They have been changed! They were washed clean from those sins. And the same is true for you. If you have done something that you feel guilty or ashamed about, know that God can and will forgive you if you repent of your sin and seek his forgiveness. You are not ruined for life. You can start over, you can have a clean slate, you can begin again.

And the last step for living out God's plan for sexuality is to understand that we all need help! We can't do it on our own. Temptations are everywhere—we need the encouragement of other Christians to help us keep our commitments to live out our sexuality in the way God intends. A great thing to do is to develop an accountability relationship with an older Christian friend or mentor. Find someone you can trust who will encourage you in your faith and pray for your courage to face sexual temptation. Speak honestly and frankly with that person about your struggles. Get real about what you're dealing with, and invite that person to give you advice and help you make right choices. And you may think I'm crazy to say this, but another way to get help is to talk to your parents. Sure, it feels uncomfortable to talk to your mom or dad about sex, but by being honest and open about questions you have, you'll discover that they were once teenagers, too! They want the best for you and can help you navigate these rough waters with their love and encouragement.

# Wrapping Up

*Set up four pillar candles in the front and dim the lights in the room.*

Let's wrap up our meeting with a time of prayer. Each time I light a candle, I will tell you something I'd like you to focus on as you pray. You will then have some time to pray silently about that area. You may pray with your eyes open or closed.

*Light the first candle.*

Dear God, we focus on the truth that you created sexuality. You created sex to be good—to be a passionate expression of love within the bounds of marriage. Help us develop a biblical view of our own sexuality. Wipe away from our minds the distorted messages about sex that we've received from the world.

*Allow time for teenagers to pray silently. Then light the second candle.*

God, we focus now on the issue of sexual abstinence. We know that you want us to wait until marriage. That isn't always easy, God. We ask now that you help us make a heartfelt commitment to wait, and that you help us set healthy boundaries.

*Allow time for students to pray. Then light the third candle.*

God, we focus now on your forgiveness of sexual sin. We're so glad that you love us and forgive us! If we've messed up, we confess our sins

## TIP FOR THE LEADER

Here are some additional Scripture passages you might want to share that contain principles applicable to sexuality: Proverbs 4:23; 6:25-26; 1 Corinthians 6:9-11; 7:8, 32-35; 2 Corinthians 12:9-10; 1 Timothy 5:1-2; 2 Timothy 2:22; and James 4:7-8.

to you. We pray that you help us start over. Also, we all pray that you help us to not be judgmental of those who have committed sexual sin, but instead to show them grace and kindness.

*Allow time for silent prayer. Then light the fourth candle.*

God, we focus now on our need for help. Help us learn how to talk with our parents, mentors, and Christian friends about our questions and concerns related to sexuality. Give us the courage we need to be upfront and honest. Empower us to ask for help.

*Allow time for silent prayer. Then say "amen."*

*Ask students to open their eyes, and give each teenager a small candle with a drip guard. Invite them to prayerfully come to the front and light their candles from one of the four pillar candles. When everyone has a lit candle, continue the message.*

God is our source of light and truth. Through prayer, Christian encouragement, and applying the Bible to our lives, God will light our way and guide our steps in the area of sexuality.

*Lead the group in a final prayer.*

God, you made us as sexual beings and you have a great plan for our lives. Be a light to us as we commit to live out your plan for our sexuality. Help us find our way through dark times and confusing questions. Let your good plan for our lives shine brightly so that others can see your love and truth. In Jesus' name, amen.

*Have students extinguish their candles.*

## DAILY CHALLENGE®

*Have teenagers form same-gender groups of three to five students. If possible, have an adult leader of the same gender join each small group. Invite groups to discuss these questions, being sensitive to teenagers who would like to keep their thoughts on this sensitive subject private.*

*Ask*

- **What stood out to you the most from this message? Why?**

- **What one thing will you commit to doing in order to live out God's plan for your sexuality?**

*Before students leave, remind them to follow through on their Daily Challenge commitment—and to tell someone how it goes.*

# The Dirt on Sharing Your Faith

## TOPIC
**Sharing Faith**

## SCRIPTURE
- Matthew 9:35-38; 13:1-23

## PURPOSE
To encourage students to create environments where they can share their faith.

## SUPPLIES NEEDED
- *Essential Messages* CD
- Bibles
- Table
- Two 2x4 pieces of wood, any length
- Hammer, nails, and measuring tape
- Plants or flowers
- Index cards and pens
- Dry-erase board with dry-erase marker, or newsprint, tape, and marker
- Small boxes filled with soil (one box for every five to six students)
- Four pieces of poster board and four sets of color markers

## SET-UP
- Print enough of the "Cultivating the Hearts of Others" handout from the *Essential Messages* CD for every five to six students to have one.
- Set up a table near the front of the room, and place two groups of items on the table: (1) the construction items and (2) the plants or flowers.

### TIP FOR THE LEADER

If possible, be sure the soil in each box includes some of the following items: small rocks or pebbles, weeds, sticks, dirt clods, pine cones, and so on.

## Starting Off
### The Dirt on Sharing Faith

*Have students form groups of three to four, and give each group an index card and pen. Each group should assign one person to be the "recorder" and one person to be the "spokesperson." Gather students around the table you set up before the meeting, and give groups four minutes to record their thoughts on the following assignments:*

• Come up with as many one-word adjectives as you can for the construction elements.

• Come up with as many one-word adjectives as you can for the plant elements.

*Bring everyone back together, and ask spokespersons to share. Then ask the following question:*

*Ask*

• **How are the items in these two groups alike?**

• **How would you sum up the differences between the items?**

One group was comprised of construction items that are nonliving and that are used to build nonliving structures. The other group was comprised of organic items that are alive and come from the environment. Many Christians believe that sharing faith is primarily about *constructing* a list of facts and *building* arguments. And while this approach has its place, creating an *environment* that encourages growth is even more important.

Sharing our faith is primarily about the environment we create in which to do it. That's just what we're going to focus on today.

# Digging In

*Read aloud Matthew 9:35-38. Then lead a short discussion.*

*Ask*

• **What do you think Jesus is referring to when he speaks about the harvest and the harvest field?**

• **Why do you think Jesus reacted to the "harassed and helpless" crowds by identifying this particular need?**

Jesus clearly saw that the people needed leaders to help and guide them. He followed up almost immediately with a very practical response; as recorded in the very next chapter of Matthew, Jesus sent his own disciples into the "harvest field." With that context in mind, let's look at the "dirt" on sharing our faith. In other words, let's explore what kind of environment we need to nurture in order to grow a good harvest.

## Good Soil Is Essential

*Have students form groups of five to six. Give each group a box of soil.*

Preparing the soil is the most important action we can take to create an environment that is conducive to sharing our faith with others. Take a few moments to run your fingers through your group's box of soil.

*Have groups discuss the following questions and then share their answers with the larger group:*

*Ask*

- **What would you have to do to prepare your group's soil for planting?**

When it comes to preparing the soil for sharing our faith, there are two very practical tips we should follow. The first practical tip is to make sure we plow our soil.

*Ask*

- **Why is plowing before planting so important?**
- **What kinds of debris would you need to plow through in your life in order to prepare to share your faith with others?**

The second practical tip that will help us create an environment conducive for sharing our faith is preparing the soil of others.

*Ask*

- **What do you think preparing the soil of others would require?**

In Matthew 13:1-23, Jesus used another organic illustration to talk about the condition of people's hearts and their responsiveness to his good news. This passage can help us understand how to prepare the hearts of others to hear what we have to share about our faith.

 *Distribute a "Cultivating the Hearts of Others" handout from the* Essential Messages *CD to each group. Explain that each section of the handout represents a person who you may share your faith with. Ask groups to read the Scriptures and discuss the questions. Afterward, have groups share a bit about their insights under each section.*

By plowing our own soil and cultivating the soil of others, we create good soil in and around our lives—the kind of soil that is conducive to sharing our faith.


## Growth Comes in Cycles

But good soil is only one element to creating the right environment for sharing our faith. Timing is another important element. When do we listen and when do we speak? When should we share and when should we just be present? When do we sow and when do we reap?

It's important to remember that spiritual growth often comes in cycles or seasons. In other words, people's spiritual journeys go through seasons just as the natural world does. This means that effective "faith sharers" know how to recognize the seasons in their own lives and in others' lives.

For instance, if someone is in a spring season, new spiritual growth is occurring. This person might not be really close to Jesus yet but is beginning to think about a relationship with him.

Someone in a spiritual summer season is experiencing significant growth.

Be sure students understand that they can share their faith in ways other than simply speaking. For example, someone in the spiritual winter season likely will be turned off by a presentation of the gospel. Instead, the best approach for this person might simply be to live out your faith. As this "winter" person emerges from the winter season into a spring season, he or she is much more likely to be open to both the gospel message and the messenger.

For a person in a spiritual fall season, spiritual interest is beginning to cool off.

Finally, if a person is in a winter season, he or she may have no interest at all in spiritual matters or a relationship with Jesus. As faith-sharing people, it's important that we appropriately approach or respond to people in each season. We have to let God guide us in how we uniquely treat each person—though always with love and authenticity.

*Have students form four groups—a winter, spring, summer, and fall group. Give each group a piece of poster board and a set of markers. Ask each group to draw a person who represents its assigned spiritual season. The picture should have as many descriptive elements as possible. For example, a picture of someone in the spiritual fall season might include headphones to illustrate that the person is listening to something other than God's Word.*

*Also ask groups to list two ways they might approach their assigned person to share their faith. Give groups six minutes to complete this assignment.*

*Afterward, have one person from each group hold up the poster the group created and someone else from that group describe the poster and their ideas about how to share their faith with the person depicted in the poster. Then lead a short discussion.*

*Ask*

- **How do these posters make you think or feel?**

- **How do they teach us how sharing our faith is affected by someone's spiritual season?**

- **How can this help us create a better environment in our lives for sharing our faith?**

# Wrapping Up

*Have students return to their original groups of five to six, and be sure each group has a box of soil again.*

Remember, building techniques and constructive strategies for sharing our faith are essential. But Christians who effectively share their faith also understand the "dirt" on sharing faith. They understand that the environment they create for faith sharing is just as important as the skills or techniques of faith sharing.

As we've said, it's important to know the condition of our own soil before cultivating the soil in someone else's life. As I ask the following questions, spend a few moments quietly reflecting on what season you are in.

*Ask the following questions, pausing for 30 seconds between each question. Considering playing soft, contemplative music in the background during this segment.*

*Ask*

- **Which spiritual season do you think you are currently in? Are you satisfied with this season? Would you like to change seasons? How?**

*Pause.*

- **How is your season affecting the way you share your faith?**

*Pause.*

- **How can you create an environment in your own life that makes you more open to hearing what others have to say about their own faith?**

*Pause.*

- **How can you create an environment in your life to help you better share your faith with others?**

*Pause.*

*Give students time to pray in their groups about the condition of the soil in their own lives and the condition of the group's soil. As they pray, have them pass around the box of dirt and run their fingers through the dirt. When they have finished praying, have them answer the Daily Challenge questions below.*

# DAILY CHALLENGE®

*Ask*

- **What one thing will you commit to doing to create an environment in your life that is conducive to sharing your faith with others?**

- **What one thing can we do together as a group to create an environment in your life that is conducive to sharing your faith with others?**

*Before students leave, remind them to follow through on their Daily Challenge commitment—and to tell someone how it goes.*

## PARENT CONNECT

Sometimes God uses pain in people's lives to create an environment of openness to the good news. Develop a handout with the following questions for teenagers to take home and discuss with their parents.

- What is the purpose of pruning a plant?

- How has God used pain to prune bad things out of your life?

- How has God's pruning created health in your life?

- When we experience God's pruning, how can we best respond?

# The Ultimate CLOG Remover

## TOPIC
**Sin**

## SCRIPTURE
- Psalm 40:8
- Proverbs 1:29-31; 24:30-34
- Matthew 19:16-23
- Luke 9:62
- Acts 3:19
- Hebrews 10:22
- James 1:25; 2:17; 3:16

## PURPOSE
To help students recognize sin, turn away from it, and choose to do what leads them closer to Jesus.

## SUPPLIES NEEDED
- *Essential Messages* CD
- Bibles
- Two-gallon bucket; canning funnel; two pitchers of water; and items to clog the canning funnel opening such as tennis balls, rags, large pieces of produce, and so on.
- Pens
- Plunger, plumbing snake, and bottle of Drano

## SET-UP
- Print enough copies of the "Your Guide to CLOGS" handout from the *Essential Messages* CD for each student to have one.
- Set up a table near the front of the room with the following items: two-gallon bucket; canning funnel; two pitchers of water; and items to "clog" the canning funnel opening such as tennis balls, rags, large pieces of produce, and so on.

---

### TIP FOR THE LEADER

If your group is large—more than about 15 people—consider running this "clog experience" experiment in smaller groups of six to eight people.

## Starting Off

*Have students gather around the table where you've set up the bucket, canning funnel, and so on. Ask one volunteer to hold the canning funnel over the two-gallon bucket. Demonstrate how water flows freely into the bucket through the funnel. Then ask several other volunteers to take turns placing different objects such as a tennis ball, large piece of produce, and a rag into the mouth of the funnel. With the addition of each item, pour water into the funnel's mouth to study the flow of water through the blocked funnel.*

## CLOGS Cause Backup

Today we are examining what causes clogs in our relationship with Jesus and how the Holy Spirit can help us deal with these clogs.

*Ask*

- **In real life, what causes clogs in a sink or bathtub?**
- **What happens to the water? to the sink or the bathtub?**
- **How is this like what happens in our lives when we sin?**

When we sin, it's similar to developing CLOGS in our lives. It causes a break in our relationship with Jesus, and our spiritual life becomes stagnant and contaminated.

# Digging In

In order to effectively deal with clogs in our relationship with Jesus, we must first recognize what clogs look like to see if any are developing in our lives. Let's use the acrostic CLOGS to look at sins that commonly clog people's lives.

 *Distribute a pen and a copy of the "Your Guide to CLOGS" handout from the* Essential Messages *CD to each student, and let them know that they'll be referring to it periodically throughout the message.*

## Recognizing the CLOGS in Our Lives

The C in CLOGS stands for "choice." Every choice we make brings us closer to or moves us further away from God. Plus choices build upon one another, making it difficult to change directions once we have started going down a particular path.

*Have students form groups of four to five to discuss these questions:*

*Ask*

- **What are examples of good choices and poor choices teenagers make?**
- **How do choices build upon one another—what does that mean to you?**
- **How can choices building upon one another be a good thing? How can it be a bad thing?**

*Read aloud Proverbs 1:29-31. Ask groups to discuss these questions:*

*Ask*

- **How would you rephrase these verses in your own words?**

- **How have you seen the truth in this Scripture demonstrated in real life?**

We are responsible for any sinful choices we make because many opportunities exist to listen to the good advice of others. What's more, sooner or later we face the consequences for those choices.

*Have students refer to the area of the handout that pictures the fruit. Ask group members to work together to identify, for each piece of fruit, a consequence of sin. After a few minutes, have volunteers share a few consequences that their groups identified.*

So here's a question for you to ponder: Are your choices bringing you closer to Jesus or taking you away from him?

*Give teenagers approximately 30 seconds to silently think and pray about this question.*

The L in CLOGS stands for "laziness." Through his life, death, and resurrection, Jesus has done everything necessary for us to have a relationship with him. But often we are too lazy to do our part in that relationship through activities such as prayer, Bible study, and interaction with other Christians.

*Ask a volunteer to read aloud Proverbs 24:30-34. Direct teenagers to the section of their handouts where the weeds are illustrated. For each weed, have groups identify how laziness clogs our relationship with Jesus. For example, groups might name one weed "missed opportunities" to signify the fact that when we're not pursuing our friendship with Jesus, we miss opportunities he puts in our lives to serve him and others.*

*Give groups about five minutes to work, and then ask volunteers to explain some of the weeds they thought of.*

So here's a question to ponder: Have you been so lazy in your relationship with Jesus that weeds are sprouting?

*Give teenagers approximately 30 seconds to silently think and pray about this question.*

*Ask a volunteer to read aloud Matthew 19:16-23, and then have groups discuss these questions:*

*Ask*

- **Do you think money and possessions are sinful? Explain.**

- **How can money and possessions clog our friendship with Jesus?**

The O in CLOGS stands for "objects," which often become a more important priority in our lives than Jesus. If our lives are more about getting and keeping *stuff* than about loving and serving the Lord, we've got a big, gooey clog.

So here's a question to ponder: Have any objects become a higher priority in your life than your relationship with Jesus?

*Give teenagers approximately 30 seconds to silently think and pray about this question.*

This message could easily be divided into two messages. If you'd like to do so, this is the natural ending spot for the first message.

*Read aloud Hebrews 10:22, and then ask groups to discuss these questions:*

*Ask*

- **How does guilt affect your life? your friendship with Jesus?**

- **Why do you think confession helps to free us from guilt?**

The G in CLOGS stands for "guilt." It's important to understand that we are all guilty because we are all sinners. But Jesus forgives us, makes us new, and removes the clog of guilt from our lives. Even so, we continue to battle with sin. So when we talk about a "guilty conscience," we are referring to the shame we feel when we do not regularly confess our sins. Without confession—which means recognizing that you've sinned, apologizing, and resolving to remove the sin from your life—the clog of sin grows and rots our "plumbing."

So here's a question to ponder: Is unresolved guilt clogging your friendship with Jesus?

*Give teenagers approximately 30 seconds to silently think and pray about this question.*

As a way to wrap up everything we've discussed so far, the S in CLOGS stands for "self-centeredness." Self-centeredness is the root of all sin. Simply put, clogs develop when we want our way over God's way.

*Read aloud James 3:16.*

Before moving on, let's take a minute to think about the clogs developing in our lives. Spend some time in silence and, on the space in your handout, record the two categories of CLOGS that you struggle with the most.

The first step to dealing with CLOGS is to recognize the sin that has developed in our lives. But recognition is not enough. We must take the second step.

**(Refer to Tip for the Leader on this page.)**

## Remove Sin and Restore Relationship— With Drano

Let's examine ways to unclog a pipe.

Have students gather around you. Pass around a plunger, snake, and bottle of Drano. Ask volunteers to name and demonstrate how to use each item. Then ask this question:

*Ask*

- **What are the differences between these items in terms of the effort we have to expend to remove a clog?**

When it comes to unclogging sin in our lives, the Holy Spirit works more like Drano than like this snake or plunger. It's not that there is no required effort on our part—the Bible tells us to fight against sin and flee temptation.

However, the Bible also states that God, through the Holy Spirit, is the one who conquers sin. We have to choose to use the "Drano," but the Holy Spirit does the work of actually removing the clogs.

So how do we open ourselves up to the work of the Holy Spirit? Again, let's use an acrostic to help us see how God removes clogs from our lives and restores our friendship with Jesus. The acrostic we'll use is DRANO.

 *Have students refer to the "Your Guide to CLOGS" handout.*

The first step to cleaning out clogs in your life is desire, which is what the D in DRANO stands for.

*Ask a volunteer to read aloud Psalm 40:8. Then ask the group to define "desire."*

Desire could be defined as a deep longing or wish. When we desire something, we crave it and pursue it no matter what. If you don't develop a desire to do God's will, it will be difficult to deal with clogs. Christianity doesn't work without a strong desire to follow Christ—that's what Christianity means. As Ron Hutchcraft says, "Christianity is like suntan lotion...it only works if you rub it in."

So here's a question to ponder: Does "desire" describe your relationship with Jesus?

*Give teenagers approximately 30 seconds to silently think and pray about this question.*

The R in DRANO stands for "repent." As you develop a desire to follow Jesus, you also will develop a desire to repent of your sins.

*Read aloud Acts 3:19. Then ask teenagers to discuss what is meant by the word "repent." To demonstrate what "repentance" means, have students stand up, move away from any furniture or other obstacles, and face the same direction. Explain that they are to march forward until you call out "about face!" At that command, they are to plant their feet and then pivot around before continuing to march.*

*Have students begin marching forward, and call out "about face" every few seconds. Then have teenagers return to their seats.*

Repentance literally means a total change in direction. It is turning away from something and toward something else. In this case, it is turning from sin and turning toward God. It's doing more than saying you're sorry; it's asking for forgiveness *and* allowing God to control that area of your life.

So here's a question to ponder: Is full repentance—that total change in direction—a regular part of your life?

*Give teenagers approximately 30 seconds to silently think and pray about this question.*

The A in DRANO stands for "actions." In the unclogging process, it's important to remember that actions speak louder than words. To get rid

## BONUS IDEA

During this time of quiet mediation and reflection, play soft, prayerful music. Also have several adult mentors on hand, stationed at different areas throughout the meeting space, to talk with, pray with, and counsel any teenagers who need it. Be sure to utilize adult mentors who can respond appropriately to teenagers' concerns about the sin in their lives.

Explain CLOGS and DRANO in your next parent newsletter. Challenge parents to reflect on their own CLOGS, and encourage them to discuss the CLOGS and the DRANO process with their teenagers. This should provide great opportunities for significant spiritual conversations within families.

If you want to take this a step further, host parents and deliver this message especially for them. Throughout the message, help them apply what they're hearing not only to their own lives, but to their families' lives as well.

of CLOGS, we must do more than say we want to change—we must start allowing Jesus to change us.

*Read aloud James 2:17. Then have students form groups of four to six. Ask each group to develop a one- to two-minute skit demonstrating how actions speak louder than words. Don't give too many instructions so that teenagers will use their creativity. However, if groups need help, here are a few ideas: (1) parent making a promise to a child, only to break it, (2) person pretending to listen to a friend while actually watching TV, (3) person on the phone begging a parent for money while at the mall buying frivolous stuff. Give groups about five minutes to prepare, and then have each group perform the skit. Applaud each group's performance.*

So here's a question to ponder: What do your actions reflect?

*Give teenagers approximately 30 seconds to silently think and pray about this question.*

Once we repent from sin and start acting in line with our beliefs, are we to constantly worry about the past? No! Once we've learned from the past and changed our behavior accordingly, we should develop a "no looking back" mentality. That's what the N in DRANO stands for.

*Read aloud Luke 9:62.*

*Ask*

- **What do you think it means to live life without looking back?**
- **What difference do you think it would make in people's lives if they stopped agonizing over past mistakes?**

"No looking back" means we learn from past mistakes, but we don't dwell on them so much that they cripple us. It means that we focus forward, toward what God has in store for us.

So here's a question: Are you living life without looking back?

*Give teenagers approximately 30 seconds to silently think and pray about this question.*

Finally, the O in DRANO stands for "ongoing." We must always remember that the Christian walk is ongoing.

*Ask a volunteer to read aloud James 1:25. Then discuss this question:*

*Ask*

- **What is this Scripture telling us?**

We will blow it from time to time. We will need to walk through the DRANO process regularly to keep clogs from developing. This is why prayer, reading the Bible, talking with other Christians, and other supporters to your faith are so important. Your friendship with Jesus is just like any other friendship—it's an ongoing relationship that must be protected and nurtured.

# Wrapping Up

Have students refer to the two CLOGS they wrote on the handout under "My Toughest Clogs." Ask them to privately select one CLOG and walk through the DRANO process in their minds. After about five minutes, instruct students to close their time of reflection in silent prayer.

Finally, to demonstrate how God uses the DRANO process to unclog the sin that holds back their relationship with Jesus, instruct students to hold up their handouts, make a small tear at the dotted line, rip the section titled "My Toughest Clogs" from their handouts, and tear up those CLOGS and throw away the pieces. Lead students in a prayer, thanking God for removing CLOGS from their lives.

## DAILY CHALLENGE®

Reflect on the experience you just had.

*Ask*

- **Which one or two elements in the DRANO process is the hardest for you to follow? Which are the easiest? Why?**

Have everyone choose a Daily Challenge they'll follow through on in the days that follow.

*Ask*

- **What is one way you can build one step of the DRANO process into your daily life?**

Before students leave, remind them to follow through on their Daily Challenge commitment—and to tell someone how it goes.

# 16 Esther, the Stress Buster

1/22/12

## TOPIC

**Stress**

## SCRIPTURE

- Esther 1:1–4:17
- Philippians 4:6

## PURPOSE

To help students look to God and the Bible for ways to deal with stress in their lives.

## SUPPLIES NEEDED

- *Essential Messages* CD
- CD player
- Bibles
- Paper, marker, masking tape
- Five medium-heavy objects such as rocks, hardcover books, or hand weights
- Two or three sturdy bedsheets
- Several "relaxation" objects such as a stress ball, a massage tool, and an aromatherapy candle

## SET-UP

- Set up the CD player with the *Essential Messages* CD cued to track 8, "Fast-Forward."

- Write the numbers "1" through "10" on 10 pieces of paper; then tape them in numerical order spread out along a wall in your meeting room.

- Test the durability of the bedsheets by layering them on top of each other, putting all the heavy objects in the middle, and then pulling the edges together to create a bundle. Lift it over your shoulder and hold it for a while, making sure the objects aren't so heavy that they cause the sheet to rip. The bundle should feel fairly heavy, but not so loaded down that it would be impossible for a teenager to hold. Also get some friends to help you test laying the sheets out on the floor and picking the objects off the floor by lifting up the edges of the sheet. Again, make sure the objects aren't so heavy that they cause the sheet to rip.

## Starting Off

Let's look at a "typical" day in the life of a teenager.

*Get 10 to 20 student volunteers and assign them the following roles:*

*Sarah (teenage girl)*

*Shauna (pre-teen girl)*

*Courtney (teenage girl)*

Michael (teenage guy)

Mr. Jones (high school teacher)

Mom (Sarah and Shauna's mother)

Dad (Sarah and Shauna's father)

Jeremy (teenage guy)

Jeremy's friends (up to 4 guys)

Cheerleaders (up to 8 girls and/or guys)

*(If you have fewer than 10 students, assign each student multiple roles.)*

*Explain that the volunteers are going to act out a skit without any rehearsal. They just need to listen to the narrator (on the CD) and do whatever is described. They should also add their own motions and facial expression to represent the dialogue they hear. Have all the actors stand offstage until their character is mentioned in the skit.*

*Play the "Fast-Forward" skit on the CD (track 8). After the skit, lead a short discussion.*

*Ask*

- **Can you relate to Sarah in this skit? Why or why not?**
- **Which part of Sarah's day seemed the most stressful? Why?**
- **What are other common causes of stress for teenagers?**

## Life Can Be Stressful

As we saw in this skit, life can be pretty stressful. We all face varying degrees of stress on a daily basis. The teenage years are a particularly stressful time. You may be dealing with academic pressure, high expectations in sports, countless hours of practicing a musical instrument, negative peer pressure, being teased or bullied, conflict with your parents, and negative relationships with siblings. On top of all that, you wish you were dating, wish you looked different, wish you got more sleep, wish you had less homework, and wish you had more money. Even faith can cause stress—you may feel pressured to pray more, serve more, share more, give more, and be more.

Ugh! The good old days of being a stress-free 6-year-old were great, weren't they?

# Digging In

Think about your own life over the past couple of days. How stressful has it been? What has stressed you out? What situations have you been dealing with?

I'd like you to rate your level of stress over the past few days on a scale of one to 10. A one means "no stress" while a 10 means "extremely stressful."

*Give students a minute to privately decide on their stress level; then point out the numbered papers you taped to the wall. Explain that students should indicate the number they chose by standing in front of it.*

*Form small groups of two to six students by grouping teenagers together with those who rated their stress levels similarly. If possible, try to create at least one really stressed group, one moderately stressed group, and one stress-free group.*

Let's work together to dive deeper into the topic of stress and the effects stress can have in our lives. I'd like you to discuss some questions in your small groups; be prepared to summarize your conclusions for the rest of us.

*Have small groups discuss these questions:*

*Ask*

- **What have been the main causes of stress in your life over the past couple of days?**

- **What are the effects of stress on a person's physical health? Have you experienced any of these effects? If so, when?**

- **What impact can stress have on personal relationships? When has stress impacted one of your relationships?**

- **How can stress negatively affect a person's faith development? Can it have a positive effect on faith? If so, how?**

*Invite a representative from each small group to briefly summarize their conclusions; then make some observations about how the various groups' answers compared or contrasted with one another.*

We all face stressful situations in our lives. Some of us are smack dab in the middle of major stress right now. Today we're going to look at someone in the Bible who is an awesome example of how to deal with stress.

*Layer two or three bedsheets on the floor. Then summarize Esther 1:1–4:8.*

Did you catch all that? Here is an orphaned Jewish girl, minding her own business, when she is forced to join a king's harem. (*Place a mildly-heavy object such as a rock, a large book, or a small hand weight in the middle of the sheet.*) She has to keep her Jewish identity a secret because it could endanger her life. (*Place another object in the center of the sheet.*) Esther is chosen as queen, which sounds great...until we consider the fact that her husband, the king, was the same guy who kicked out his last wife because she wasn't "obedient" enough! (*Place another object in the center of the sheet.*) Soon Esther and her cousin Mordecai learn that Haman, one of the highest royal officials, is planning to murder all the Jews in the land. Remember, this includes Esther. (*Place another object in the center of the sheet.*) So Mordecai comes up with a plan: Esther will talk to the king. But I forgot one small detail:

## BONUS IDEA

After small groups share their summaries of the effects of stress, give them some more info about the physical and psychological effects of stress. You can find medical information about the impact of stress on the body and on psychological behavior by doing a search on these Web sites:

http://my.webmd.com

http://www.stress-and-health.com

http://health.discovery.com /encyclopedias

If you're working with middle school– or junior high–aged students, ham things up at this point by prompting students to face a partner. When they're all looking eyeball-to-eyeball, give them this challenge: How do you think Esther felt at this point? You've got one second to put your face and body into a pose that represents how stressed you think she felt. Ready? Go!

Teenagers will get a kick out of their partner's exaggerated poses. After a moment, tell them to look around the room at the other students, while still trying to keep their faces and bodies frozen.

Applaud their crazy, dramatic efforts, and then continue the message.

Anyone who approached the king's throne without being summoned was executed. *(Place another object in the center of the sheet.)*

- **How would you rate the stress level of Esther's situation on a scale of one to 10? Why?**

I'd rate Esther's situation a ten: She's married to a husband with a temper, her entire cultural group is about to be wiped out, and the solution to the problem lies on her shoulders. And if she *tries* to help, she's likely to get killed!

*Pull together the corners of the sheet and lift the heavy bundle off the floor. Grasp the sheet in such a way so as to make it like a bag. Invite a volunteer to be "Esther" and have him or her stand up front next to you and hold the bag over his or her shoulder. (Be careful not to select a superstrong weight lifter as your volunteer! Instead, choose someone who is of average size and strength.)*

Esther was carrying quite a load of stress! Let's see what Esther did.

*Invite a volunteer to read aloud Esther 4:9-17.*

*Ask*

- **What observations can you make about how Esther got through this stressful situation?**

We can learn a lot from the way Esther dealt with stress.

## Prayer Is Essential When Dealing With Stress

Esther didn't sit down and chart out a detailed five-part plan for dealing with the situation. She didn't freak out. She didn't try to de-stress by pounding an extra-large pepperoni pizza. When the rubber met the road, the first thing Esther did was turn to prayer. She really believed prayer would make a difference! Esther prayed and fasted for three days. We don't know for certain what she prayed about, but I imagine a lot of it was just talking to God about her fears, asking for courage, praising God for his power, and relying on him to give her strength.

When you face stressful situations, you, too, should turn to God in prayer.

*Read aloud Philippians 4:6.*

When anxiety-producing problems threaten to overwhelm you, just pray. Pray about anything and everything. Tell God what's on your heart. Thank God for his presence in your life. Pray, pray, pray.

## When You're Stressed, Turn to Other Christians for Support

Esther didn't just pray by herself; all the Jews in the region prayed along with her! She relied on the community of God to come alongside her. Esther wasn't afraid to ask for help—she knew she couldn't do it on her own. Her community of faith responded to her call for help and supported her 100 percent.

When we're stressed out, we often make the big mistake of trying to deal with it on our own. Yeah, we might pray to God about it, but ask other people to help us deal with it? No way!

The sad truth is that when we try to make it on our own, we're cheating ourselves. God designed us for community, and he created the church to be a family that can support and encourage one another. Like Esther did, we need to rely on our community of faith to help us through stressful times! Don't ever be afraid to tell a Christian friend that you need prayer. That's what we're here for!

## Lean on Your Family in Times of Stress

From Day One, Esther's cousin Mordecai had her back. Since she was an orphan, he adopted her as his own daughter. He loved her very much. He also challenged her to step up to the plate. We can see in Esther 4:13-14 that it was Mordecai who called Esther to be a brave and courageous woman of God, to take a risk, and to become the hero who would save her people. And when the going got tough, Esther knew she could rely on Mordecai. She trusted his counsel and asked for his prayers. Esther knew Mordecai would be there for her, no matter what.

When you face stress, turn to your family for love and encouragement. Don't let conflicts or awkwardness hold you back from talking to your parents or other relatives about what is going on in your life. Ask them for advice and for prayer. *They love you!* They want to help you get through the tough spots in life. And your family members, like Mordecai, will help you step up to the plate. They'll encourage you to stretch and challenge yourself because they want you to be the best you can be. When you rely on your family for courage and support, you won't feel so alone as you tackle the stress in your life.

*Turn to "Esther" and say:*

Your load would be a lot lighter if you had help, wouldn't it?

*Invite the volunteer to put down the bundle; then have everyone gather around and hold on to an edge of the layered sheets. When everyone is holding on to part of the sheets, lift the sheets and heavy objects up together.*

### TIP FOR THE LEADER

If "Esther" is having a hard time holding up the bag while you speak, that's OK. Just challenge him or her to keep trying. If it has become way too heavy, let the student rest the base of the bag on the floor. This will still be a great object lesson, demonstrating that it is often way too hard to carry a load of stress on our own.

Create a newsletter to send to your teenagers' parents. Share some data with them about the symptoms and effects of stress (see Web sites such as http://www.aacap .org/publications/factsfam/66.htm or those mentioned in the Bonus Idea on p. 99). Let them know that today's generation of teenagers is really stressed out!

Prompt parents to consider the level of stress in their student's life: Is their child overscheduled? overtired? under a lot of pressure? Is their child's emotional health, personality development, relationship development, or physical health being damaged by stress? In your newsletter, suggest that parents do something fun that is entirely focused on helping their teenager de-stress. Suggest several ideas, such as:

• Sending a teenager to a movie with friends;

• Drawing a bubble bath and providing "spa" supplies;

• Letting a teenager sleep in on a Saturday morning then serving him or her breakfast in bed;

• Or, in cases of extreme stress, sanctioning a day off from school to have some health-giving time with Mom or Dad by playing board games together, reading books, watching a movie, and taking a nap.

Some of your students' parents may be overly stressed, too, so include a suggestion that they apply one of these ideas to their own lives.

Though prayer can help us a great deal, if we never turn to others for encouragement and support when we're facing stress, we'll still be carrying a heavy burden on our own.

But when we turn to others—to Christian friends and to our family members—we discover that our load has become much lighter! They are alongside us, helping us carry our burden and easing the stress in our lives. The contents on this sheet haven't changed, but when we hold them together, it's a lot easier. Similarly, though friends and family members usually can't take away the tough situations we face, when we share our burdens with them, they can help us carry the load.

*Have everyone take a seat; then continue.*

## Realize That You Can't Control the Results—Just Trust God

Imagine how Esther felt when she said the words, "If I perish, I perish." She wasn't exaggerating—she knew she could very likely be killed for what she was about to do! But she reached a point when she realized that she couldn't control the results of the situation; she just had to trust God and do what she knew was right.

This may be one of the hardest steps in dealing with stress, but it's also one of the most important. We can double or triple our stress load by worrying incessantly about how things will turn out. "What will she think when I say that?" or "Will he hate me when he's heard what I've done?" or "What if I don't get that job?" or "What if I get hurt?" There are countless possible negative or positive results to every situation. You've got to realize that no matter how hard you try, *you can't control the results*. There's one thing you *can* do, though—you can trust God. He is in control. And even if the worst happens, you can trust that God is with you. Be like Esther, who faced the possibility of death with courage because she trusted God no matter what.

You might be wondering what happened with Esther. Well, the good news is that God got her through this level-10 stress bonanza. When she approached King Xerxes, he was compassionate toward her and decided not to execute her. In fact, she was eventually able to talk to the king about Haman's evil plan. The Jewish people were saved! And remember cousin Mordecai? He got a promotion: he became King Xerxes' right-hand man.

Let's spend some time experiencing three of these important ways to deal with stress: prayer, relying on Christians for support, and determining to trust God.

*Have teenagers form trios and take a few minutes to talk to one another about stressful situations they're facing. Then prompt them to pray together, asking God for help and determining to trust him no matter what happens.*

## Decide *Not* to Contribute More Stress to Your Life

In addition to prayer, relying on Christian friends and family members, and trusting God, we also need to evaluate the circumstances that are causing the stress in our lives. Esther didn't have a choice about the stressful circumstances she was placed in, and some of us don't either. For example, your parents may be going through a divorce—you don't have any control over that. No matter how much you wish it were different, you can't change the situation. There are lots of other stress-causing situations that we can't control.

But the truth of the matter is that there are other times when we actually contribute to the stress in our lives. We create circumstances that pile on the stress until we can't take it any more.

*In trios, have students talk again about the skit from the beginning of the lesson using these two questions:*

*Ask*

• **Which causes of stress didn't Sarah have any control over?**

• **Which causes of stress *did* Sarah have control over?**

Let me tell you a true story. In 2003, accomplished hiker Aron Ralston was exploring some canyons in Utah. The 27-year-old was hiking alone when an 800-pound boulder crashed down on him, crushing his arm and pinning him in a dark crevasse. Ralston was stuck—nothing he did would move the boulder. No one knew where he was. He quickly ran out of food and water, and his body started to go into shock. He was certain he was going to die.

On the sixth day trapped in the crevasse, Ralston did the unthinkable: He broke his own arm then used a small knife to cut it off. Yes, that's what I said: He cut off his own arm. The pain was unreal, but he knew he had to do it or he would die. After amputating his arm, he hiked for four hours until finding someone to help him. Unbelievably, Ralston survived.

Like the huge boulder that crushed Ralston's arm, stress can literally or figuratively kill us. Stress can cause life-threatening health problems. Stress can kill our joy, our peace, our personality, and our spiritual lives.

When it came down to it, Ralston was willing to cut off his own arm to save his life. It hurt terribly, but he knew it was what he had to do. There may be circumstances you have control over that are trapping you in stress. You may be involved in too many activities. You may have friends who are adding stress to your life or having a negative influence on you. You may be watching or listening to things that make you anxious or angry. You need to ask yourself a tough question: What do *I* need to cut out of my life in order to reduce the stress?

It may hurt. It might mean giving up a favorite sport or saying goodbye to a friendship. But you can't let stress trap you. You need to be willing to cut those stressors out of your life.

# Wrapping Up

*Pass around the "relaxation" objects you gathered, such as a rubber stress ball (the kind people squeeze in their hands), a massage tool, or an aromatherapy candle. Explain what each object is and the purpose it serves.*

Each of these items can help a person de-stress and relax...on the surface. Though it might feel nice to relax a bit, none of these objects will truly deal with the stress in a person's life. The only real help for stress is to put into practice the steps we learned from Esther: turning to God in prayer, relying on our community of faith, leaning on our families, and putting the results in God's hands. We can also defeat stress by changing our stress-causing circumstances when it's possible.

Esther knew how to bust stress. Though you may not face a dramatic situation like hers, you *can* overcome the stress in your life and impact your world in amazing ways.

## DAILY CHALLENGE®

*Have teenagers return to their stress-level small groups from the first "Digging In" activity and give the teams these Daily Challenge assignments:*

*Prompt the stress-free small group(s) to discuss ways they can minister to people who are stressed. Challenge them to each decide on a specific action they'll take this week to encourage a stressed-out person.*

*Have the moderately stressed group(s) discuss the application points (prayer, Christian community, family, and leaving the results in God's hands). Ask them to each share which area they most need to grow in and how they'll put that into action.*

*Direct the really stressed group(s) to talk about the application points as well as their need to "cut off" stressors from their lives. Prompt them to each commit to a specific action step to help them dial down their stress levels.*

*Before students leave, remind them to follow through on their Daily Challenge commitment—and to tell someone how it goes.*

# Oops, I Did It Again

*4/22/12*

## TOPIC
**Temptation**

## SCRIPTURE
- Matthew 6:13
- 1 Corinthians 10:12-13
- 1 Timothy 6:6-14

## PURPOSE
To help students identify sources of temptation in their lives and develop practical ways to handle them.

## SUPPLIES NEEDED
- *Essential Messages* CD
- Bibles
- A variety of items to give students as gifts (one for each student, plus extras): inexpensive items such as candy bars, a few nicer items such as cool pens, and a couple of even cooler items such as CDs.
- Magazines, newspapers, and other media items including printouts from Internet search engines such as the Yahoo! home page (http://www.yahoo.com), an e-zine home page, or a blog home page; a TV; and a radio (The TV and radio should be plugged in so they function.)
- Paper and pens
- A bottle of vitamins, a hand weight, sunblock, a smoke detector, and a fire extinguisher

## SET-UP
- Print enough copies of the "Charting Temptation" handout from the *Essential Messages* CD for each student to have one.
- Hide the gifts you've collected so teenagers can't see them. Keep the extra gifts in a separate bag.
- Set up several stations in the room: one with a TV, one with a radio, and one with print and Internet media.

## Starting Off
### What's Behind Door Number 3?

*Explain that you're going to play a game. Give each student one of the gifts you brought in. Explain that students can choose to keep their items or trade them with someone else's (that person also must agree to the trade). After any trades have taken place, ask again if anyone wants to trade. For all those who want to trade, they must exchange their gifts with the person directly to their right. After this, allow anyone*

## TIP FOR THE LEADER

A measured degree of vulnerability can be a good way to introduce tough topics. Students may be touched by your sharing of a time when you gave in to temptation, but you don't want a story of failure to distract them from the promise that they can face and overcome temptation.

who wants to keep his or her gift to sit out. Then ask if anyone still wants to trade. For those who do, take their gifts away and give them another gift—from the ones that had been hidden from them—instead. (Some of these gifts should be more valuable than what you initially gave out—a dollar bill, for example, and some should be less valuable.) Some teenagers will end up with a better trade, and some won't.

In our lives, there are always things that will tempt us to give up what we have for something else. Sometimes it will seem like a valuable trade, and sometimes we'll realize we made a costly sacrifice.

*Lead a short discussion.*

*Ask*

- **What tempted you to give up what you had for something else?**

- **What was it like to make a trade?**

- **How is that similar to the way temptation sometimes works in real life?**

- **How are we sometimes tempted to make sacrifices that don't involve material things—for example, giving up a relationship with a friend because of someone else?**

 *Have students form pairs, and make sure each pair has a Bible. Have pairs read 1 Timothy 6:6-14 together and then discuss the following questions:*

*Ask*

- **What does this Scripture mean to you?**

- **How does it relate to the activity we just did?**

- **How can contentment keep us from temptation?**

- **How do you think you can develop contentment in your life?**

# Digging In
## What Appeals to You?

The first step to dealing with temptation is learning to identify the things that are trying to tempt you.

*Point out the three stations you set up throughout the meeting area: TV, radio, and print/Internet media. Distribute paper and pens, and explain that students are to move from station to station. At each station, they should study the media available, list the different ways the media could tempt someone, and answer the question "What do the media use to persuade people?" When everyone understands, allow students five to 10 minutes to complete the activity.*

*Ask*

- **What types of temptation do you see in the media?**

- **Do you think the temptations are effective? Explain.**

*Distribute the "Charting Temptation" handout from the* Essential Messages *CD. Explain that students will complete this chart individually, using the graph to identify how much each of the listed temptations weigh upon them. After two to three minutes, have teenagers fold their papers so no one can see their answers and gather together. Then lead a discussion.*

*Ask*

- **Did anything on the graph surprise you? Why?**

- **What makes you aware of the kinds of things that create temptation for you? When are you not aware?**

- **How do you "fight the good fight of faith," as the Scripture passage says, when you face temptation?**

- **Where is Jesus when you are being tempted?**

*Have a volunteer read aloud Matthew 6:13.*

When we pray, "Deliver us from the evil one," God tends to start with the evil that is within our own hearts rather than protection from someone else's evil behavior.

*Ask*

- **Why do you think "Lead us not into temptation" and "Deliver us from the evil one" appear side by side in this prayer?**

- **Why might God want to start by delivering us from the temptation within our own hearts?**

 Let's take a moment to offer to God the things that tempt us.

*Allow a couple of minutes for silent prayer. You might play meditative, prayerful music while students pray.*

 Temptation is everywhere. Just turning off the TV isn't enough to avoid it. The Timothy passage told us that "godliness with contentment is great gain." Instead of hoping that we never run into temptation, we are better off if we content ourselves with things that God wants us to have and pray that we won't desire anything else.

## Fireproofing Your Life

Once we've clearly identified sources of temptation, the next practical measure is to prevent ourselves from getting into places where we can be tempted.

There are actually as many concrete ways to prevent temptation as there are ways to prevent house fires. We're going to use some objects to jog our thinking about how to prevent temptation.

*Use a creative object lesson to bring this point home. Show various preventative medicines and measures (vitamins, exercise equipment,*

---

**TIP FOR THE LEADER**

Object lessons can be fun memory makers. When you refer back, at a later date, to the items you used, teenagers will more easily recall what they learned.

*sunblock); and preventive measures people take to keep their homes safe (a fire extinguisher and smoke detector). Pass these objects around and discuss what they help to prevent.*

Temptation is harder to resist directly than to avoid preventatively. In other words, once you're already surrounded by temptation, it gets a lot harder to deal with than if you think ahead. Imagine going on a diet and deciding that you're not going to eat any ice cream—while you're standing in the ice cream store. It would be a lot harder to resist than if you decided before you walked in.

Once we are in the face of temptation, we find ourselves pulled toward it. So if we can prevent ourselves from being near it, we're more likely to avoid it.

*Ask*

• **What are some practical ways to avoid temptation?**

• **What makes them easy? What makes them difficult?**

• **How might temptation affect your friendship with Jesus?**

In our lives, we need...

• smoke detectors—things that remind us that we are being tempted;

• fire extinguishers—things that help us escape temptation when we face it;

• insurance—the reminder that God will forgive us when we give in to temptation; and

• a "neighborhood-watch program"—friends who will help us stick to the values God wants for our lives.

Let's go through each one and call out examples that would work for our own lives.

*Go through each of these four categories (and any others you would like to add) and have students call out (1) something that could help them recognize temptation, and (2) something that helps them turn away from temptation.*

## God Forgives Us When Temptation Gets the Best of Us

Temptation is common to everyone. Rather than living with guilt, it is important to remember that God forgives us. We may leave today with the best of intentions to avoid temptation. But as we saw at the beginning, the media keeps temptation constantly before our eyes. Even if we could turn it all off, anyone who wants to make a buck off of the public will most likely use all kinds of temptations. We can never totally avoid it. Consequently, we will sometimes give in. Remember that God loves you no matter what temptations you've given in to. The Bible tells us that nothing can ever separate us from Jesus' love for us.

*Invite students to find a place in the room where they can be alone. Have them each take their "Charting Temptations" handout, a pen, and a Bible with them. Have teenagers silently read 1 Corinthians 10:12-13 and then, on the back of their handout, write an honest letter to God about temptation, struggle, and hope.*

# Wrapping Up

Everyone knows about temptation, and everyone knows they have sometimes given in to it. Jesus loves us no matter what we've given in to. He's also eager to help us avoid temptation. What we don't so often think about is that you can prepare yourself for temptation ahead of time and face it with more preparation than you might have otherwise.

## DAILY CHALLENGE®

*Ask*

- **Have you discovered anything new about temptation?**
- **What will help you see, avoid, and deal with temptation when it happens to you?**

*Have everyone choose a Daily Challenge they'll follow through on in the days that follow.*

*Ask*

- **What one thing will you commit to doing to avoid temptation this week?**
- **Who can best help you follow through on your commitment?**

*Before students leave, remind them to follow through on their Daily Challenge commitment—and to tell someone how it goes.*

### BONUS IDEA

Bring in a guest speaker from Alcoholics Anonymous (or another recovery group or ministry) who can talk about how giving in to temptation took over his or her life.

### PARENT CONNECT

Have students carry forward the object lesson at home. First suggest that they observe how their homes have been protected (through insurance, alarms, locks, and so on). Have students walk with their families around the home, pointing out the various ways the home is protected. Then families can discuss how they can protect themselves and one other from temptations that hurt the family.

# Who Do You Trust?

## TOPIC

**Trusting God**

## SCRIPTURE

- 1 Kings 18:19-39

## PURPOSE

To help students vividly understand that they can trust God with their whole hearts, 100 percent of the time.

## SUPPLIES NEEDED

- *Essential Messages* CD
- CD player
- Bibles
- Blindfold
- Bible commentaries on the book of 1 Kings (or photocopies of pages commenting on 1 Kings 18:19-21 from one commentary)
- Toy basketball and basketball hoop (or trash can)
- Items that represent common teenage idols (money, a mirror, sports equipment, a diploma, keys, a video game, a CD, and so on)

## SET-UP

- Set up the CD player with the *Essential Messages* CD cued to track 9, "There's More to the Story: Part One."
- Set up an obstacle course in your meeting area. It can be a simple course using chairs, tables, and other items already found in your space.
- Set up the toy basketball hoop or trash can.

## BONUS IDEA

Tell a "trust breaking" story. Think of a funny, lighthearted story of how a family member or friend broke your trust. For instance, did someone ever forget to pick you up at the airport? Did anyone ever stand you up for a lunch appointment? Be sure to only use a lighthearted story—it is unwise to share something that will embarrass or shame others.

## Starting Off
### Who Do You Trust?

Who or what can you trust 100 percent of the time? Here's a trust-building game with a bit of a twist.

*Ask for two volunteers to leave the room, and give them the blindfold; tell them that when they're called back in, one person is to be blindfolded.*

*Send the volunteers out of the room. When they're gone, tell the rest of the group that the two volunteers will be completing the obstacle course when they come back in, with the blindfolded person relying on instructions from the non-blindfolded person. The job of the rest of the*

The point of these questions is to help teenagers realize that no mortal human can be trusted 100 percent. Depending on circumstances, motivations, perceptions, mistakes, and unforeseen conditions, even trusted friends will disappoint us. What's more, expecting someone to never disappoint us is unfair. Mortal humans are flawed; therefore, even those with good intentions will occasionally disappoint us.

group is to shout out improper instructions to the blindfolded person.

*Have the two volunteers return, and explain that they're to complete the obstacle course as a team, with the blindfolded person relying on verbal instructions from the non-blindfolded person. As the volunteers begin navigating the course, encourage the rest of the group to shout out the improper instructions. Afterward, ask the two volunteers these questions:*

*Ask*

- **How did each of you feel during this exercise?**

- **Who did you trust? Why?**

*Then lead a short discussion with the entire group.*

*Ask*

- **What does if feel like to have someone break your trust?**

- **What does it feel like for you to break someone's trust?**

- **Who in your life can you trust 100 percent to never let you down? Explain.**

- **Who do you always follow no matter the circumstances? Why?**

# Digging In
## The Challenge

*Ask several volunteers to share the responsibility for reading aloud 1 Kings 18:19-39.*

This sounds like an intense story. But the story starts much earlier than 1 Kings 18. Listen to this!

*Play "There's More to the Story: Part One," track 9 on the* Essential Messages *CD. Afterward, lead a short discussion.*

*Ask*

- **What factors made this conflict grow in intensity?**

- **Put yourself in Elijah's shoes: How do you think he felt in the midst of the conflict? What emotions was he probably experiencing?**

- **Have you ever experienced a situation that caused you to have similar emotions?**

When Elijah said, "Stop wavering and choose who you will follow," he was basically saying, "Who do you trust? Which God will you depend on?" He is throwing down a major challenge to King Ahab and the people of Israel.

*Have teenagers form groups of three or four.*

*Ask*

- **How would you summarize the challenge Elijah gave to the people?**

- **What might Elijah's challenge to the church today sound like?**

- **What might Elijah's challenge to you sound like?**

## The Contest

After throwing down the challenge, Elijah proposed a contest between God and Baal to settle once and for all which God was real, trustworthy, and dependable. Let's examine the guidelines and rules Elijah set up for the contest.

*Have a volunteer read aloud 1 Kings 18:22-25.*

Do you see what is happening here? Elijah, to prove Yahweh was the only one, true God who could be trusted 100 percent, did *not* make the contest fair. He gave every benefit to the prophets of Baal! Let's make sure we understand exactly what Elijah was trying to do.

*Have students take turns trying to shoot baskets into the basketball hoop or trash can you set up, using the following rules: Students must try their first couple of shots from 10 feet away from the basket and with the hand they* don't *use to write with. Then students can try their next couple of shots one to two feet away from the basket using the hand they write with. After this exercise, discuss the following questions:*

*Ask*

- **How was this experience similar to the contest Elijah set up with the prophets of Baal?**

- **Why do you think Elijah gave all the advantages to Baal's team?**

## The Competition

So Elijah threw down a challenge, proposed a contest, and then he let God prove himself in head-to-head competition with Baal in verses 27-39.

 *Play "There's More to the Story: Part Two," track 10 on the* Essential Messages *CD. Afterward, lead a short discussion.*

*Ask*

- **How sincere do you think the prophets of Baal were in their belief that Baal would produce fire?**

- **How do you think the results of their efforts affected their trust in Baal?**

- **Have you ever sincerely trusted in someone or something only to be disappointed? If so, how did you feel?**

- **How does God's trustworthiness rate in this account?**

- **What makes something or someone trustworthy?**

### TIP FOR THE LEADER

To help students really dig in to the background of the passage, you may want to distribute commentaries on 1 Kings 18:19-21 (or photocopies from the same commentary); then continue with a discussion.

Some teenagers will never have used a Bible commentary before and might be intimidated. You may want to take a few minutes to explain how to use the commentary, how commentaries are developed, and why they can be helpful in biblical study and spiritual growth. By utilizing such tools during messages, you can develop your teenagers' lifelong Bible study skills—and, therefore, help them grow a stronger friendship with Jesus.

In your next parent newsletter or at your next parent meeting, use the story of this showdown to bring up the topic of trustworthiness with parents. Encourage parents to think about how they can create an environment in their homes where (1) God can prove himself trustworthy (through praying for specific family needs, for example); and (2) they can prove themselves trustworthy (by following through with commitments made to their children).

# Wrapping Up

*Place the items that represent common teenage idols at the front of the room. Allow students to choose items and name what idols they represent in today's teenage culture. Then lead a discussion.*

*Ask*

- **Why do people trust these items—what do these things promise to provide?**

- **What modern-day "idols" are you tempted to trust?**

- **Do these things follow through with their promises—do they prove trustworthy? Why or why not?**

- **How have these items "broken" trust?**

- **Compare God's trustworthiness to the trustworthiness of the idols these items represent.**

- **How can we develop the kind of trust in God that Elijah had—a 100 percent–kind of trust?**

## DAILY CHALLENGE®

The question for each of us is how long will we waver, dance, or hop between two options? Who will we choose to trust?

*Have teenagers form groups of three or four and discuss the following questions:*

*Ask*

- **How do you think Elijah's trust in God developed over time?**

- **Do you believe God is trustworthy? Why or why not?**

- **What are some ways to develop trust in God?**

- **What are some steps you can take to develop trust in God?**

*Have everyone choose a Daily Challenge they'll follow through on in the days that follow.*

*Ask*

- **What one thing will you commit to doing this week that will allow God to start proving his faithfulness to you in head-to-head competition with your idol?**

*Have students pray for one another within their groups. Specifically, ask them to pray that they would be open to God's faithfulness, especially concerning their Daily Challenge.*

*Before teenagers leave, remind them to follow through on their Daily Challenge commitment—and to tell someone how it goes.*

# (19) Jesus' True Identity

12/18/11

## SCRIPTURE

- Isaiah 7:14; 53:2-6
- Micah 5:2
- Matthew 1:18–2:1; 5:3-10, 38-42; 16:13-16; 25:34-40
- Luke 10:30-37; 23:26–24:8
- John 3:16; 8:42-59; 10:14-39; 15:15

## PURPOSE

To help students get to know the "real" Jesus and understand how to grow in a personal friendship with him.

## SUPPLIES NEEDED

- *Essential Messages* CD
- Bibles
- 48 pieces of construction paper, markers, and masking tape
- Additional construction paper (one piece per teenager) and art supplies such as markers, glitter, scissors, glue, crayons, and paint

## SET-UP

- Print a copy of the "Claims and Accomplishments Quiz" from the *Essential Messages* CD.

- Print several copies of the "Quotes About Jesus" from the *Essential Messages* CD. Cut apart the quotes so you have one copy of each quote for every student.

- Use the "Claims and Accomplishments Quiz" to create a game board on the wall of your room. Write each clue and answer on a separate piece of construction paper. Tape the answers to the wall in rows (to look like a TV game-show board) in any order you'd like. Then tape the clue sheets atop the corresponding answers.

# Starting Off
## Trivia Game Show

Welcome! We're going to start out with a trivia game show, so get your brains ready!

*Divide teenagers into three or four equal teams and point out the construction paper game board that is taped to the wall. Explain the rules this way:*

Each of these pieces of paper has a clue written on it—either a great accomplishment or an amazing claim that a person from history or current times has made. When it's your team's turn, you should decide together which clue you want to pick. Your team then gets one chance to quickly guess the name of the person who made that claim or did that accomplishment. After you've made your guess, a member of your team should walk up to the game board and remove the clue sheet to reveal the answer underneath. After the answer is revealed, the next team has a turn to guess. We'll keep playing until all of the clues have been guessed.

*When everyone understands how the game will be played, clarify that you aren't keeping track of points—it's just for fun.*

*Lead teenagers in playing the game, and ham it up in your role as game show host. Applaud teams for their efforts on each turn. The game is concluded when all of the clue sheets have been removed and the correct answers have been revealed. Lead a discussion after the game. Ask:*

- **In your opinion, which of these accomplishments is most amazing? Why?**
- **Which claim is most unusual? Why?**
- **Which person on the wall do you admire most? Why?**
- **Who do you admire the least? Why?**
- **Which were the toughest to guess?**
- **How were you able to identify the people you guessed correctly?**

Today we're going to examine the identity of someone who had the most amazing accomplishments and made the most world-rocking claims in human history: Jesus.

# Digging In

There are a lot of opinions about Jesus in our world today.

*Lead a short discussion. Ask:*

- **What do most of the people at your school think of Jesus?**
- **What other opinions about Jesus have you heard?**

 *Distribute a copy of "Quote 1" from the "Quotes About Jesus" handout to each student. Invite a volunteer to read the quote aloud.*

Some people think Jesus never existed.

*Lead teenagers in a short discussion. Ask:*

- **How common is this point of view among people you know?**
- **Do you agree or disagree with this opinion? Explain.**
- **If someone shared this opinion with you, how would you respond?**

## Jesus: A Historical Figure

Jesus is not a figment of someone's imagination. Nearly all historians and scholars agree that Jesus was a real historical figure. In addition to the New Testament Gospels, some of which contain eyewitness accounts of people who knew Jesus, several ancient historical documents outside of the Bible attest to his existence. Jesus was born around 4 B.C. during the reign of Herod the Great in Palestine, now modern-day Israel. Let's read how the Bible describes his birth.

*Invite a volunteer to read aloud Matthew 1:18–2:1.*

He began his public ministry around the age of 30. Some of Jesus' most famous teachings have impacted 2,000 years of human society. Let's read some of his most well-known teachings.

*Invite volunteers to read aloud Matthew 5:3-10; 5:38-42; 25:34-40; and Luke 10:30-37.*

Clearly, Jesus existed as a human being who lived upon this earth. We can see the impact of his life and words on our world today.

Let's look at another opinion about Jesus.

*Distribute a copy of "Quote 2" from the "Quotes About Jesus" handout to each teenager. Invite a volunteer to read the quote aloud.*

Some people, like these characters in *The Da Vinci Code*, think Jesus was just a good human being—not the Son of God.

*Lead teenagers in a short discussion. Ask:*

- **How common is this point of view among people you know?**

- **Do you agree or disagree with this opinion? Explain.**

- **If someone shared this opinion with you, how would you respond?**

## Jesus: The Son of God

The problem with this quote from *The Da Vinci Code* is that it's just plain wrong. Jesus *did* claim to be the Son of God. Let's examine some of the things Jesus said.

*Invite volunteers to read aloud John 8:42-59, and 10:14-39.* (me)

We can see clearly in these passages and many others that Jesus claimed to be the Son of God. This consistent message so angered the Jewish religious leaders that they tried to have him killed. And eventually Jesus *was* brutally executed for his "blasphemy."

Countless biblical writers attest to Jesus' claim to be the Son of God, many of his followers were executed for believing Jesus' claim, and Jesus himself was crucified because of it. When we consider this quote from *The Da Vinci Code,* we simply need to use basic logic: If Jesus *hadn't* claimed to be divine, then the Jews would have had no grounds to execute him.

Let's look at one more Scripture passage.

*Invite a volunteer to read aloud Matthew 16:13-16.*

Here Peter, one of Jesus' followers, boldly declares that Jesus is the Son of God. Earlier during our trivia game, we were able to identify some famous people based on their accomplishments and claims. Similarly, Peter was just a normal guy, but as he hung out with Jesus, he saw Jesus' amazing accomplishments and miracles: Jesus made lame people walk, blind people see, and he had even raised dead people back to life. Peter had seen Jesus calm a raging storm with one command and multiply a few fish and loaves of bread into a meal for five thousand people! Peter also heard Jesus' spectacular claims, such as calling God his Father, using the phrase "I Am," which is how God identified himself in the Old Testament. When Peter observed Jesus' accomplishments and claims, he knew in the very core of his heart who Jesus really was: the Son of God.

Let's look at a third opinion about Jesus.

*Distribute a copy of "Quote 3" from the "Quotes About Jesus" handout to each student. Invite a volunteer to read the quote aloud.*

Some people recognize Jesus as the promised Messiah and Savior of the world.

*Lead teenagers in a short discussion. Ask:*

• **How common is this point of view among people you know?**

• **Do you agree or disagree with this opinion? Explain.**

• **If someone shared this opinion with you, how would you respond?**

## Jesus: The Prophesied Savior

There are hundreds of prophecies in the Old Testament that describe a coming Messiah. They describe what the Messiah will be like and what he will do. Some of the prophecies contain amazing details. And the amazing thing is that Jesus fulfills every one of them. Let's read some of them.

*Invite volunteers to read aloud Micah 5:2 and then Isaiah 7:14; 53:2-6.*

We can see clearly that these prophecies describe Jesus—he was born in Bethlehem and his mother, Mary, was a virgin. Later, as Isaiah 53 describes, Jesus was beaten and suffered greatly when he took our sins upon himself and died on the cross.

It's no mere chance that Jesus fulfills all the hundreds of prophecies in the Old Testament. Let's forget that there are hundreds of prophecies for a minute—let's imagine there were just eight. The chance of any random person fulfilling just eight of the Old Testament prophecies is one in 10 to the 17th power. Do you have any idea how infinitesimally small that chance is? According to the book *Evidence that Demands a Verdict* by Josh McDowell, it would be like covering the entire state of Texas with silver dollars, piled two feet deep. One of those silver dollars would be painted red. Then imagine you were blindfolded and were able to wander around the whole state of Texas. You got one chance to bend down and pick up a silver dollar, hoping it would be the right one. The likelihood of your picking up the red coin on your first try is the same likelihood of a person just happening to fulfill eight Old Testament prophecies. And don't forget—Jesus didn't just fulfill eight, he fulfilled *them all.*

Jesus was God's Messiah who was born on Earth not just to rescue the Jewish nation, but to rescue all of humankind from sin. All of us are sinners, and our sin separates us from God. But when Jesus died on the cross, he took all our sin upon himself and paid the penalty we deserved. Three days later, he rose from the grave, showing his victory over sin and death.

*Invite several volunteers to read aloud Luke 23:26—24:8 and John 3:16. (me)*

Jesus, the prophesied Savior, died for *you*. He took your sins upon himself when he suffered and died in your place. He loves you! When you believe in him, you can find forgiveness for your sins and eternal life with Jesus in heaven. Jesus can save you from your sins.

Let's look at a third opinion about Jesus.

*Distribute a copy of "Quote 4" from the "Quotes About Jesus" handout to each student. Invite a volunteer to read the quote aloud.*

Some people view Jesus as their friend.

*Lead teenagers in a short discussion. Ask:*

- **How common is this point of view among people you know?**

- **Do you agree or disagree with this opinion? Explain.**

- **If someone shared this opinion with you, how would you respond?**

## Jesus: Friend

Jesus is the Son of God and the prophesied Savior of the world. How amazing is that! But in John 15:15, we see Jesus describe himself in another very important way.

*Have a volunteer read John 15:15 aloud.*

Jesus called his followers *friends*. Wow! Just think about that for a moment—they had a *friendship* with the Son of God!

What's your relationship with Jesus like? Is it distant or nonexistent? Is it based only on logic or tradition—just acknowledging what you've learned in church without taking it any deeper? Do you know that you can also call Jesus your friend? You can have a loving, growing, personal relationship with Jesus. You can talk to Jesus about your life through prayer. You can get to know him better through studying Scripture. You can know him in a meaningful way.

If you don't have a friendship with Jesus, you can begin one. You can pray, asking Jesus to forgive you of your sins and inviting him to be your friend. If this is something you want to do or that you have questions about, please come talk to me after we wrap up our meeting.

For those of you who are Christ-followers, what is your relationship with Jesus like? Do you regard it as a friendship? Are you focused on knowing Jesus more and more each day?

E-mail parents, challenging them to set aside some time this week to talk with their teenager about their own faith story. How did they come to the understanding that Jesus was their Savior? How has their relationship with Jesus made a difference in their lives?

Teenagers will benefit from hearing about their parents' journeys of faith and will be inspired to live out their own journeys with Jesus.

# Wrapping Up

As we read earlier, Jesus asked Peter, "Who do you say I am?" We've read several quotes that have answered that question differently. The fact of the matter is that we all need to answer that same question for ourselves. Who do we say Jesus is?

*Set out art supplies and construction paper.*

I'd like you to think for a moment about how you personally answer that question. Then I want you to express your answer to the question using art. Take a piece of construction paper and decorate it in any way you'd like to answer the question from Jesus: "Who do you say I am?" You can focus on one of the points we've learned about, or you could go in your own direction of prayer or praise.

*Allow time for teenagers to each complete their creative expressions (using pictures, words, symbols, etc.). Then explain that they should each go to the trivia game board and remove a piece of paper then use tape to replace it with their piece of art.*

You've just created an awesome mosaic of praise, showing who Jesus really is. When you hear all the opinions about Jesus that are floating around, remember this mosaic and take confidence that you know the truth. Jesus is a real historical figure who walked upon this earth. He is the Son of God and the prophesied Messiah. He is the Savior, who died on the cross for our sins and rose from the dead. And Jesus is our friend. We can know him personally and intimately.

## DAILY CHALLENGE®

*Have everyone stay gathered around the mosaic.*

As you look at this representation about what we believe about Jesus, take some time to pray silently about how you'll apply this to your life. Perhaps you need to begin a friendship with Jesus or you've realized you want to grow closer in your relationship with Jesus. Or perhaps you need to tell your friends about Jesus. Whatever your life application step is, pray about it now.

*Allow time for prayer, and then have teenagers form pairs. Ask*

- **What one thing will you commit to doing in response to what you've learned about Jesus?**

*Before teenagers leave, remind them to follow through on their Daily Challenge commitment—and to tell someone how it goes.*

# 20 Worshipping the Way God Wants

## TOPIC
**Worship**

## SCRIPTURE

- 1 Samuel 15:22
- Psalm 51:16-17
- Proverbs 21:2-3
- Hosea 6:6
- Amos 5:21-24
- Micah 6:6-8
- Romans 12:1

## PURPOSE

To help students discover that they can worship God by the way they live each day; and to challenge them to express worship in meaningful ways, both privately and publicly.

## SUPPLIES NEEDED

- *Essential Messages* CD
- CD player
- Bibles
- Musical instruments and sheet music
- Robe, beard, sandals, or other "Old Testament prophet" costume supplies
- 3 sheets of newsprint, markers, masking tape
- TV, VCR/DVD player, and *Never Been Kissed* video/DVD (Flower Films/Fox 2000 Pictures, 1999)

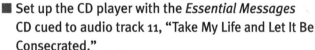
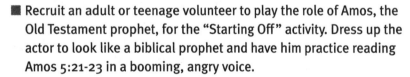

## SET-UP

- Print enough copies of "A Living Sacrifice" handout from the *Essential Messages* CD for each student to have one.

- Set up the CD player with the *Essential Messages* CD cued to audio track 11, "Take My Life and Let It Be Consecrated."

- Recruit an adult or teenage volunteer to play the role of Amos, the Old Testament prophet, for the "Starting Off" activity. Dress up the actor to look like a biblical prophet and have him practice reading Amos 5:21-23 in a booming, angry voice.

- Set up a TV and VCR/DVD player, and cue the movie *Never Been Kissed* to 1:38:00 (if you're using a VCR, set the counter to 0:00:00 when the studio logo appears). Preview the clip at least once before teenagers arrive.

- Tape three large sheets of newsprint to the wall of your meeting room.

## Starting Off
### God *Hates* Worship?

Worship. What does it mean? What is its purpose? Today we're going to explore what the Bible says about worshipping God.

*Invite teenagers to form small groups of three or four to discuss these questions:*

*Ask*

- **What is the best worship experience you've had over the past couple of years? Describe it.**

- **What made it meaningful to you?**

*While teenagers are discussing these questions, ready any song leaders and instruments. Make sure the Amos actor is ready and waiting outside the room.*

Let's start out by worshipping God right now.

*Lead the group in singing a favorite worship song. When the song is about two-thirds of the way through, the Amos actor should run into the room and up to the front, yelling angrily: "I have a message from God! I have a message from God!"*

*Stop the song. When all eyes are on Amos, he should loudly read Amos 5:21-23 from his Bible. When he's done reading, Amos should leave the room.*

Thanks, Amos. Now let's think for a moment about what Amos just said. God spoke through this Old Testament prophet and, as you heard, he used really strong language—words like *hate* and *despise*—against people just for worshipping him with music, offerings, sacrifices, and religious festivals. Why in the world would God *hate* his people's worship?

# Digging In

The text we just heard from Amos 5 addresses some of the most common ways of worshipping God in the Old Testament times. Some of the ways they worshipped God were very different from what we do today: They worshipped God through making animal sacrifices, fasting for set time periods, and celebrating traditional festivals. Other things they did to worship God were similar to what we do today: They gave offerings, prayed, and sang songs of worship.

Obviously, based on what we just heard from Amos, something had gone terribly wrong with the way the people were worshipping. God actually hated and despised their acts of worship!

We need to ask a basic question: if God didn't like their acts of worship, what kind of worship *did* God want? Let's look at the words of Micah, another Old Testament prophet.

*Invite a volunteer to read aloud Micah 6:6-8.*

Micah makes it exceedingly clear that true worship isn't found in animal sacrifices or offerings—what God wants is a life that's focused on honoring him.

Amos makes the same point. Let's read the full passage that we heard a bit of earlier.

*Prompt a teenage volunteer to read aloud Amos 5:21-24.*

Based on Amos and Micah, it's pretty clear that the Israelites needed to redefine their understanding of worship—and we need to do the same thing today.

## Our Daily Living Is the *Highest* Form of Worship

When we started our meeting, I asked you to share with one another about the best worship experience you've ever had. Most of you probably mentioned musical worship, great prayer times, meaningful retreat experiences, and stuff like that. I bet none of you mentioned the time you helped out at the homeless shelter by scrubbing toilets.

Just like the Israelites in the Old Testament, people today often have a mixed up understanding of what worship really is. First and foremost, worship means honoring God through the way we live our lives. Let's look at some clear examples of this principle in Scripture.

*Have volunteers read aloud 1 Samuel 15:22; Psalm 51:16-17; Proverbs 21:2-3; Hosea 6:6; and Romans 12:1. Then invite teenagers to sum up all the worship actions mentioned in the passages—write those actions on the first sheet of newsprint affixed to the wall.*

These worship actions from the Bible are a great start. But let's add some more ideas to our list—what are some other ways to worship God with our lifestyles? Shout out your ideas and I'll add them to our list.

*Prompt students to brainstorm lots of ideas and list them on the first newsprint sheet. Affirm teenagers' ideas as they share them.*

Worship means obeying God and acknowledging him in all we do. It means repenting of our sins with a broken heart and seeking forgiveness. Worship means showing mercy to others, standing up for what is right, and showing justice to those who are oppressed. In the Old Testament, they sacrificed animals, but as we read in Romans 12:1, the highest act of worship is making your *life* a sacrifice. Honoring God in the way you live each day is the truest way to worship him.

## Why We Worship

Let's watch a movie clip that will give us more insight into what worship is meant to be.

*Show the clip from* Never Been Kissed. *If you're using a VCR, set the counter to 0:00:00 when the studio logo appears. Begin the clip at approximately 1:38:00 when the crowd begins to cheer. End the clip at approximately 1:39:10 when the kiss ends and the couple smiles at each other.*

### PARENT CONNECT

Amos, Micah, and other Old Testament prophets repeatedly emphasized the importance of serving the poor and standing up for the oppressed as critical aspects of lifestyle worship. You can help teenagers and parents connect by organizing an opportunity for them to worship God through serving the poor and oppressed. Coordinate a parent/teenager service project that is directly related to issues of justice or poverty. Before and after the event, emphasize that participants just worshipped God in the greatest way!

So, you're probably wondering "What in the *world* does kissing have to do with worship?" No, I'm not suggesting we start smooching each other in between praise songs. But there *is* a good reason why I showed you this clip.

The Greek word for *worship* that is used in the Bible is *proskyneo* and it means "to kiss." What does kissing have to do with worship? I'll tell you.

First, a kiss involves love, affection, and commitment. Similarly, when we worship God, we are expressing our love, affection, and commitment to him.

Second, a kiss is both an inner emotional experience and an outward action. When we worship God, we are pairing together our inner emotional and spiritual feelings and experiences with outward actions. We're moving beyond private thoughts and feelings and are choosing to express those feelings in an outward way.

Third, the meaning of a kiss is recognizable by others. If you were at this baseball field and you saw this kiss take place, you'd instantly know what it meant. The meaning is clear: This couple is in love. Similarly, worship *means* something—something that others can observe and recognize. It means that we love God.

We don't worship God in order to impress others or to stir up our own emotions. Like a kiss, our worship is to be motivated by one thing: our desire to express our love for Jesus.

## How We Express Our Worship

As we already discussed, the Bible makes clear that the way we live our daily lives is the highest form of worship. In addition to living a lifestyle of worship, there are two other important areas of worship that are essential to the life of the Christian.

First is public, corporate worship. This means the type of worship you would participate in at church, in youth group, or in other gatherings of Christians.

*Invite teenagers to brainstorm corporate worship actions that they do at your church or that they've heard of other churches doing; list all their ideas on a second sheet of newsprint affixed to the wall. Keep challenging youth to come up with more ideas, making sure they've covered basics like singing songs or taking communion along with less obvious contributions to corporate worship such as giving money in the church offering or serving as musicians who accompany the church choir. When they've exhausted their well of ideas, review the list out loud.*

These are some great ideas, and some really important expressions of corporate worship. Worshipping God with other Christians is really important to all of our faith development because it reminds us that we aren't "Lone Ranger" Christians—we are part of a community of faith. And on those days when we feel grumpy or tired or frustrated at

God, participating in worship with other Christians helps us get over ourselves. It's sort of like positive peer pressure; we see the joy and love for God expressed by those around us, and somehow we discover that we've left our bad attitude behind and we're worshipping God, too! And we express worship to God with other Christians because it gives us a taste of heaven. Scripture tells us that in heaven, people from all tribes, nations, races, and languages will be worshipping God together. We will be united in our praise. It will be awesome! When we express worship with other Christians, we reflect that amazing truth that all Christians across the globe are one family in God's love.

In addition to public, corporate worship, it is essential for Christians to have times of private, personal worship. This is worship you express to God when no one else is around—it's just you and God.

*Invite teenagers to brainstorm private worship actions that they do or that they've heard of other Christians doing; list all of their ideas on a third sheet of newsprint affixed to the wall. Keep challenging youth to come up with more ideas, making sure they've covered things like personal study of Scripture, singing worship songs at home, praying, and fasting. When they've covered every idea they can think of, review the list out loud.*

These are wonderful ways to express our praise to God. When you're expressing worship to God on your own, be creative! Do things that fit your personality, that really click for you. For example, you could write a letter of praise to God or write a poem about your love for him; you could paint a picture that captures the beauty of God's creation; you could meditate on a Scripture verse that is meaningful to you; you could go on a walk with God and talk to him about your day; you could take pictures that express your love for Jesus; you could read the Psalms out loud... there are countless things you could do on your own to show Jesus how much you love him.

Sometimes we're tempted to check off the worship box after we've been to church. We've sung the songs, we've prayed the prayers, we're done for the week, right? The sad thing is that if we only worship God when we're in gatherings with other Christians, we're missing out on the personal intimacy God wants us to have with him—the type of relationship that will only grow when we also spend personal time alone with him.

Are you willing to start a habit of spending personal, private time worshipping God during the week? Are you willing to spend time once a week or each day that's just between you and God? If so, you'll be amazed at the impact it will have on your faith. As you express worship to God on your own during the week, you'll grow closer to Jesus. You'll love him more and more. You'll also be regularly reminded of the amazing truth that God is good, is awesome, is amazing! And that good, awesome, amazing God *loves you like crazy.* And as you habitually worship God, your heart will be changed. You'll be tuned in to hear God's voice and to respond to his leading in your life. You'll see the world in a new way. Your relationship with Jesus will bloom and grow.

## BONUS IDEA

Talk to your pastor about specific and significant ways teenagers can get involved in corporate worship expressions on an upcoming Sunday morning, such as singing in the choir, playing musical instruments, reading Scripture, preparing worship art for the sanctuary, preparing PowerPoint slides, and so on.

After teenagers brainstorm corporate worship ideas, share these opportunities with the group and help them get involved.

# Wrapping Up

In 1874 an Englishwoman named Frances Havergal wrote words that powerfully express what it means to be a living sacrifice, to worship God with our lives.

 *Distribute copies of the "A Living Sacrifice" handout, one to each student. Have teenagers form groups of three or four and invite them to read the text then discuss these questions:*

*Ask*

- **Which line of this hymn stands out to you the most? Why?**

- **How are you inspired to use our hands and feet to worship God? Be specific.**

- **How are you inspired to use your voice to worship God? Be specific.**

- **How are you inspired to use your money or other possessions to worship God? Be specific.**

- **How does this hymn define being a living sacrifice? What else might you add to this prayer of commitment?**

*When teenagers wrap up their small-group discussion, gather everyone back together.*

What a tragedy it would be if God said the words to us that he said to the Israelites in the book of Amos! Yet many of us just go through the motions of "worship" without understanding what true worship is. Let us instead live out the words of Frances Havergal's hymn—let every aspect of our lives be lived to worship God. Let us be true worshippers of God, as we seek to honor him in our actions, as we express our love to him with other Christians and on our own. Let's commit ourselves to be living sacrifices for him.

 *Invite teenagers to close their eyes and silently pray as you play "Take My Life and Let It Be Consecrated" (track 11) on the* Essential Messages *CD.*

# DAILY CHALLENGE®

*After the prayer, distribute markers and point out the three sheets of newsprint paper on the wall.*

Each of these posters is filled with awesome ideas for ways to worship God. I'd like you to think for a moment about how you will apply what we've learned to your life.

*Point to the first sheet of newsprint.*

How will you worship God with your lifestyle?

*Point to the second sheet of newsprint.*

How will you express your love for God in corporate worship?

*Point to the third sheet of newsprint.*

How will you express your love for God in private, personal worship?

Take a moment to make three specific commitments by circling an item on each sheet of newsprint that you want to apply to your life. Don't circle something that you already do regularly—instead choose an application step that will stretch you and grow your faith in new ways. When you've circled three items, find a partner and share with him or her what you circled and why.

*Prompt pairs to also discuss this question:*

*Ask*

- **How has your understanding of worship changed as a result of what you've learned tonight?**

*When pairs are done, wrap things up with a short prayer. Before students leave, remind them to follow through on their three Daily Challenge commitments—and to tell someone how it goes.*

# Scripture Index